Simple Pasta

Pasta made easy. Life made better.

Odette Williams

Photographs by
Graydon Herriott

TEN SPEED PRESS
California | New York

For Mum

Simple Pasta is a book of appetite and desire; of unpreened, simple, tasty recipes that you'll happily return to again and again. Along with the classics that we all crave (I'm talking to you, Cacio e Pepe and Carbonara), I'll also share new favorites to add to your repertoire. Consider these as seasonal blackboard menus. Pasta is the star, but I've also got the supporting acts: starters, salads, booze—and, of course, dessert—so you can put a killer meal together. There's nothing a home cook can't successfully pull off, and, yes, I'm going to convince you to make your own pasta. If you don't have the energy for the fresh stuff (I get it), you can always use dried pasta. Either way, pasta is primal. It's flour, water, and joy. Everyone loves it. So, put the music on, call your people, and let's roll.

Contents

Introduction: Channeling la Dolce Vita

The summer when I started working in earnest on this manuscript, I had planned to take the kids to Italy. The pandemic put an end to that; so instead, my good friend Amy and I hunkered down with our collective five kids and two dogs on Fire Island. We decided we'd manifest our own *La Dolce Vita*. Each night we rolled *a lot* of pasta as I jotted down recipe notes and the kids waited patiently for yet another 10:00 p.m. dinner. We filled our days with saltwater and aperitivo. We listened to music, dressed up for each other, and put on lipstick, even though it was going to be slurped off by linguine. After we put the kids to bed, Amy and I would sit down with a bottle of red, google "Italian villas," and daydream about travel, touch, and socializing again. The next day, we headed back into the kitchen and made pasta, yet again.

This book could have been called *Pasta, I Love You So Much It Hurts*. It's been a long-standing affair. My love of homemade pasta can be traced to a specific time and restaurant. I was a young kid growing up in a coastal steel town two hours north of Sydney, Australia. On Friday nights, my parents would take my brother and me to our local Italian restaurant, The Trieste, for dinner. They'd bundle us up in our pajamas (yes, we went in our robes and slippers) because by the end of the night, driving home with our bellies full, my brother and I would fall asleep in the back of the Kombi van and have to be carried to bed. Take me back! As kids, we picked up on our parents' relief and relaxation that only Friday evenings can bring about.

Going to the Trieste for dinner was an affordable treat that we all loved. It was a family-run restaurant with about ten Formica tables and a carpeted floor. It was BYOB. To get to the bathroom you had to walk through the kitchen, past the cook. There was a Chupa Chups lollipop stand on the bar that loomed over us, keeping children in check. We knew that if we played our cards right and behaved throughout dinner, we'd each get to choose one at the end of the night.

Those Italians knew a thing or two about parenting. My mom always appreciated how welcoming the owners were to children. This was back when there were no iPads and kids weren't always welcome at restaurants. Kids could be, well, kids: unpredictable, cranky, loving, annoying, curious, and excited all in a hot minute. I might be making this up, but I have memories of the owner allowing my brother and me behind the bar at the end of the night to help ring up the bill on the cash register.

Each week, we ordered the same thing: sizzling garlic prawns that came in a flaming-hot black skillet, spaghetti Bolognese that my brother and I split, and schnitzel for my parents. The laminated dessert menu showcased garish premade gelato that arrived rock-hard and never tasted as good as the pictures looked. Dessert was Trieste's weakest link, something I've remedied in *Simple Pasta* (and in my previous book, *Simple Cake*, come to think of it).

Dessert aside, everything in life felt right during those meals. I think such a happy childhood experience is why I adore twirling pasta and eating simple Italian food so much. I will never tire of the feeling it gives me. It's my comfort food. My escape. My indulgence. My way back to a time when life felt uncomplicated.

Sadly, a restaurant like the Trieste is almost impossible to find these days. But that doesn't mean you can't re-create the feeling of contentment (and pasta!) at home. In these pages, Italian is the starting point, but you'll also see influences from places I have lived in and traveled to. I've also been inspired by chefs and cooks who make homemade pasta exceptionally well. Their restaurants are places at which I'd happily eat every night, if I could. They don't just consistently cook delicious homemade pasta but they also fill my soul in a similar way as the Trieste.

There was Dolomiti's, the Italian restaurant where I worked in my early twenties, and I loved Old Papa's Cafe in Fremantle, too many trattorias around Sydney to name, and Frankies in Brooklyn (my local for over a decade). I could happily eat at Ignacio Mattos, Altro Paradiso any night of the week. I'm crazy for Missy Robbins's Lilia and Misi in Williamsburg. It's dreamy to sit at the bar at Via Carota in the West Village, and Flour + Water in San Francisco is our new haunt, when we can get a table. Il Corvo Pasta in Seattle was absolutely worth the hour-long wait that I made my kids suffer. Rolf and Daughters blew my mind with their seasonal pasta when we visited Nashville. These favorites have inspired me to imbue *Simple Pasta* with seasonal creativity and the feeling of making everyone welcome.

But here's the skinny, and why I had to write this book. How was it that someone who worshipped pasta had *never* made her own fresh pasta until she was forty? Now, I religiously make it for my family. Yes, it really is that easy! I'm guessing I'm not alone. Well, this is the cookbook that's going to be your gateway. Yes, *you* are going to make homemade pasta. And you are going to love it.

As well as giving you the tried-and-true classics that we all crave, I've made sure the recipes are focused, with an emphasis on produce that's either growing in the garden or available at the market. There's a wonderful improvisational nature to pasta; it's essentially a blank canvas for seasonal produce. I love that pasta can be a quick meal for one or a feast. Once you get to know these basic doughs, you will really be able to play. And for those nights when you just don't have the wherewithal for homemade pasta in you, reaching for store-bought dried pasta is just A-OK. In fact, for some recipes, it's preferred. For convenience, each ingredient list starts with the amount of pasta needed, whether fresh or store-bought.

In the end, I did make it to Italy. My daughter Opal told me, "You can't make a pasta book and not go." We photographed half the book on Fire Island, where it all began, and then took off to a villa in Marsala, Sicily, for a week. It was exhilarating to travel again. Opal was right, and so was the gelato. Collaborating and creating something from nothing, both on a barrier island and in a foreign country was magical. I hope *Simple Pasta* ignites your own wanderlust and that one of my recipes, menus, or personal anecdotes sparks an idea that you can run with and make your own. I'd do anything for a great meal and a belly laugh. It's pure pleasure and joy. My wish is for you to find this feeling within these pages.

Pasta Techniques

Kneading, resting, rolling . . . repeat after me.

KNEADING

Kneading is essential to develop the gluten in flour and to create elasticity so a dough can be rolled thinly without tearing. You'll have a craggy ball of dough at the start, but you'll end up with a silky-smooth, soft ball of dough after kneading.

Start by lightly flouring a clean, wooden work surface and knead using a wave-like motion. Drive the heel of your palm into the dough, pick it up and fold it onto itself, rotate 45 degrees, and then drive your heel back over the dough again. Repeat this for the recommended time or until the dough is smooth and supple and springs back when lightly pressed. After kneading, the dough should feel similar to fresh Play-Doh. If it feels wet and sticky, add a little more flour to your work surface and knead to incorporate. If it feels dry, spritz the dough with water from a spray bottle or drip very small amounts, a little at a time, and work it into the dough.

RESTING THE DOUGH

After kneading, shape the dough into a ball and wrap it well with plastic wrap to rest. Resting the dough, covered, allows for a more even hydration and gives the gluten time to relax before being rolled and shaped. Under a time crunch, I've been known to not let egg dough sit for the stated 30 to 60 minutes. Nothing bad will happen to the dough if you let it rest for longer than directed but always keep it in the refrigerator; well covered with plastic wrap during this step so it doesn't dry out.

Some folks like to rest semolina dough, but I haven't found it essential and usually start shaping immediately or within 10 to 15 minutes after kneading. Just make sure to keep the dough covered as you work.

ROLLING OUT THE DOUGH

Rolling out the dough creates a thin, silky sheet of pasta that can then be cut, shaped, or filled. Depending on what shape or cut of pasta you are making, the thickness of the dough will vary slightly, but the overall goal is to end up with a large sheet that is uniformly even.

By Machine

For all intents and purposes, an electric pasta-rolling machine, such as a KitchenAid mixer with pasta attachments, is a godsend. The machine makes rolling pasta easy and fast. Make sure to keep the machine at a slow speed while rolling the dough. Alternatively, a hand-cranked machine does the trick. A novice might find it easier and more manageable to feed smaller pieces of dough through a hand-cranked machine.

By Hand

The simplest way for a novice to roll pasta is to use a standard rolling pin and a lightly floured surface, preferably wooden. Roll the dough as you would a pie dough, only the end product will be much thinner. When you start out, don't go for a spectacularly large sheet, your goal is an evenly rolled, thin sheet. Whether using Basic or Large-Batch Egg Dough (see page 16), start by dividing the dough into four equal pieces to make the rolling more manageable. With this quantity, you'll end up with a sheet that's a similar size to a pizza. Don't worry too much about the shape of the sheet as you roll; its translucency and evenness are key. So, grab your rolling pin, and go for it. Sure, it's a cruder version than the method that I describe following but, at the end of the day, you hand rolled your pasta!

Using a Mattarello and Tagliere

I do want to share a traditional method using a mattarello and tagliere, that I learned from Sfoglina Julia Ficara of Grano & Farina cooking school in Rome. She earned the title of *sfoglina* for her expertise in rolling fresh sheets of pasta (sfoglia) by hand. Like any skill, rolling dough by hand takes time and practice to master. I'm still a work in progress but can

now roll out a respectable sfoglia. Julia is ergonomically efficient and all about getting food on the table to feed hungry mouths, no faffing or fiddling. Her speed prevents the pasta from drying out.

If you're wanting to roll out an ambitious, large sheet of dough, you will need two specific tools: a mattarello, an untreated wooden rolling pin that's about 40 inches long and thinner than a standard rolling pin (you can find beautiful vintage ones online), and a tagliere, a large untreated board, about 4 by 3 feet and roughly 1 inch thick, made of porous wood (like poplar, linden, birch, maple, or pine). Both the wooden surfaces of the mattarello and tagliere add a wonderful texture to finished pasta. Once you have these tools, it's time to master the technique. It's a challenge, and I'm no sfoglina but here's my version of how I do it.

To hold a mattarello, cup your hands so that your palms are resting on the top side of each end of the mattarello and your fingers are wrapped over it. (I pretend to have LEGO-shaped hands that snap around the roller.) This grip will allow your hands to move easily along the length of the mattarello and distribute pressure evenly. Use your palms to push the pin away from you and your fingers to guide it back. Think of pushing forward, rather than pressing down.

Now, lightly flour the tagliere. Place the dough in the center of the board and, using the mattarello, flatten it into a disc. Place the mattarello in the middle of the disc and push away from your body with even pressure, stretching the dough, and then draw the mattarello back toward the center. Work just the top half of the dough, you're not just rolling forward and backward but simultaneously gliding your hands along the mattarello. I was taught that this gliding movement traces the shape of the perimeter of the dough, moving your hands to meet in the middle of the mattarello as you near the top edge of the dough and then returning them to each side of the sheet as you pull back. Rolling the mattarello back and forth stretches the dough, while the gliding action helps achieve sfoglia with an even thickness. Repeat these movements about four times, rotate the dough roughly 45 degrees, and then repeat rolling and turning until you have an even sheet. Eventually the sfoglia will be too large to turn manually and you'll need to roll about half of it around the pin to rotate. From time to time, to remove any trapped air, roll the mattarello over the entire sheet without pressure.

When your sfoglia reaches 20 to 24 inches in diameter, let half the sheet nearest you (that you're not working on) hang over the edge of the tagliere and allow gravity to assist in stretching the dough. It's a dangerous game as the sheet can fall to the floor. To avoid this, use your hand to anchor the sfoglia to the board before unrolling it from the mattarello. However, when your sheet does hit the deck, consider it a rite of passage—unfurl, dust it off, and get back to work! Any tears can be repaired by gently pinching and sealing the dough and working gingerly around that area. A spray bottle of water is invaluable for repairing, rehydrating dough that has dried out, and sealing filled pasta. Spray a light mist of water about 10 inches from the top of the surface to avoid making the sheet too wet. As you get more experience, you'll gain more speed and avoid these pitfalls.

When the sfoglia is ready, it should be large, thin, and even. To check, roll half of it onto the mattarello and hold it up to the light. You are good to go if you can easily see your hand behind the unrolled part of the hanging sheet and there are no dark, uneven patches, Be kind to yourself and don't expect to nail it straight away.

FILLING AND SEALING SFOGLIA

If making filled pasta with sfoglia, you will need to take a different approach than that described on page 34. Fold the pasta sheet in half to create a crease line, then open it and roll up the bottom half. Place the filling, evenly spaced, going row by row, on the top half of the sheet. If the pasta with the fillings dries out too much, lightly mist with water. Uncurl the bottom half, lightly drape it up and over the top half, and enclose the fillings. Before you seal, push out all the air, starting at the crease line and working row by row from the middle to the edges. When all the air is removed, seal and cut the pasta.

Serving Sizes

No one wants to be taken down by a massive serving of pasta, unless you're heartbroken or life has had its way with you. Most times, I want pasta to leave me sated, not comatose. Traditionally, pasta is considered the primi course. However, the pasta recipes in *Simple Pasta* are flexible enough to be appetizers, main courses, or part of a larger meal. Here are a few helpful suggestions.

- Per person, use 3 ounces of uncooked pasta for a starter, and 4 ounces of uncooked pasta for a main. I've calculated equivalent portions of fresh and dried pasta for most recipes in *Simple Pasta*, so you can decide whether to make dough from scratch or use dried pasta instead.

- It's a bit baffling (I chalk it up to the magic of pasta), but the same amount of pasta dough can feed different amounts of people, based on how it's shaped, filled, or cut, as well as the sauce it's paired with. This is why *Simple Pasta* has different quantities of the egg dough recipe: Basic and Large Batch. Don't worry; each recipe will tell you which one to use.

- If truth be told, I prefer to make pasta for one or two people. I find it cuts down on the time spent rolling and cutting and makes finessing the finished dish easier, since you aren't juggling quite as large a quantity of pasta and sauce.

- Depending on the sauce and on how saucy you like your pasta, you may have leftover pesto, ragù, or red sauce. Never a bad thing.

- For filled pastas, I've provided serving sizes rather than the exact number of tortellini or other shapes the recipe yields. Depending on how small or large you make your stuffed pastas, the number will vary.

Tips for Cooking Pasta

Here are a few pointers that will help make your fresh (and dried) pasta life easier.

Use Prep and Cook Times as a Rough Guide
Simple Pasta's recipes don't include the time it takes to make fresh dough because almost every recipe provides options for using dried or fresh pasta. The dough recipes themselves provide approximate times, and, of course, depending on what type of cut, shaped, or filled pasta you're making, these will vary slightly.

Measure Your Flour
A digital scale is a pasta game changer and the most accurate way to measure ingredients for dough; measuring exact weights is essential for consistent results for making fresh pasta. To measure flour without a digital scale, spoon it into a measuring cup, then level it off using the back of a knife. Don't overfill or compact the flour or you'll end up with a dry dough.

Cook the Pasta in Plenty of Water
Give the pasta plenty of water (4 to 5 quarts) so it has space to roll around and cook evenly without sticking to the bottom or to itself. Cook in two batches or in two pots if needed.

Season the Pasta Water
The rookie mistake is to add too much salt to the water when cooking fresh pasta, since fresh pasta is very absorbent and can easily become too salty. Season conservatively. Dried pasta, on the other hand, can handle a bit more salt. My advice? Taste the seasoned water *before* cooking the pasta.

Stir—or Don't!
Fresh pastas and gnocchi are delicate and cook quickly, so don't meddle with them too much as they're cooking; stir only as needed. Filled pastas are fragile; maintain a gentle boil so they don't burst. Dried pastas, on the other hand, need stirring throughout their cook time.

Know That Starchy Pasta Water Is Everything
How many times have you accidentally poured the pasta water down the sink, forgetting to reserve some? I encourage you to use a large spider or

slotted spoon to transfer cooked pasta straight into the sauce. This way, you'll have warm, starchy water on hand to finish many sauces perfectly. If having pasta water isn't critical to a recipe, I ask you to use a colander instead, as there is no need to save the water.

Understand the Al Dente Spectrum

Homemade pasta is tender, so it will never be super al dente; that's your reward for making it from scratch. Dried pasta should have a little bite but still be silky. Pasta in recipes such as Carbonara (page 204) and Cacio e Pepe (page 130) should be transferred from the water to the sauce a few minutes shy of being done, since it will finish cooking in the sauce. Fresh egg dough pasta cut into fettuccine or pappardelle will usually cook in 2 to 3 minutes, depending on how thin it has been rolled. Shaped or filled pasta may take a little longer, 3 to 4 minutes. Similarly, fresh semolina pasta often needs a little longer to soften its toothsome nature, 3 to 4 minutes. Once again, this timing depends on how it's been shaped.

Splash in a Bit of Oil to Stop the Pasta from Sticking

If cooked pasta is not going straight into a sauce, add a splash of oil and toss to coat to stop it from sticking together.

Finish Pasta with Finesse

Tossing pasta with sauce and a little pasta water is best done in a pan with gently sloping, high sides that allows plenty of space for the pasta to be tossed and get well coated without it ending up on the floor. Alternatively, use a large, warm bowl to combine the warm pasta and sauce.

When in Doubt, Take It Off the Heat

Don't let the heat control you; you control it. Home cooks often get stuck over the flame and forget they can simply move the pan off the heat to quickly adjust the temperature.

Bring Back Warmed Plates

Like my nan used to do, warm your plates or bowls in the oven. This helps keep pasta glossy and warm for as long as possible.

Cooking with Kids

I haven't met a kid who doesn't like pasta, so these recipes are an excellent opportunity to get children in the kitchen and teach them how to cook one of their favorite things. I've found when kids are involved in the process, helping to roll gnocchi or peel vegetables, they tend to be more adventurous eaters. It's a gift to teach young ones a life skill they'll remember fondly. Chances are, you're modeling how they will cook and eat in the future. This cannot be underestimated.

Let's Roll: The Only Pasta Doughs
You'll Ever Really Need

Making homemade pasta oozes rustic charm; it's inexpensive and anyone can do it. My fourteen-year-old daughter is proof of this. Making pasta gets you out of your head and into your hands. I'm asking you to learn only three easy doughs: egg, gnocchi, and semolina. That's all! Things might go sideways on the first attempt—your eggs may escape the flour well, you may be hesitant to roll out the dough thinly enough, or the dough may stick or pucker when fed through the machine—but even beginner's pasta can be saved with a splash of sauce and mountains of cheese. So, fear not…it's just pasta! Once you make and taste your own homemade pasta, you'll think twice about going back to store-bought. I promise that in no time, you'll be making fresh pasta even on a weeknight. Yes. Yes, you can!

Egg Dough

This is what you've come for, the Rolls Royce of pasta. There is no definitive egg dough recipe; mine is home-friendly and uses whole eggs rather than just yolks, because who wants to be left with a bunch of egg whites? I've also found that it's easier for beginners to work with a dough that's not laden with yolks. I experimented with all sorts of flours, but it's hard to beat tipo 00 flour, a finely ground flour that results in an elastic dough and pasta with a superb mouthfeel. All-purpose flour works just fine, too, but if you want the real deal, you'll add 00 to your grocery list. I honed my pasta skills by learning from a handful of women, including Sfoglina Julia Ficara and my friend's Italian mother, Mama Sordo. Sfoglina Ficara is a pasta purist and uses only flour and eggs to make an egg dough. When these ingredients are measured accurately, the eggs alone should provide enough hydration to the flour to make the dough. My recipe is influenced by Mama Sordo, who gives the home cook a little wiggle room and often adds a bit of olive oil, salt, and water to her dough. Once you've made the dough a handful of times, feel free to have your own opinion about these additions. A stand mixer with pasta attachments makes homemade pasta so quick and easy. I use mine *all the time.* It will change your pasta game; I can't recommend it enough. But a hand-cranked pasta machine or rolling pin can also do it. Rolling egg dough by hand is a skill that is developed over time, not overnight. Once you master my basic recipe, feel free to play with variations.

Basic Egg Dough and Large-Batch Egg Dough

A general rule of thumb:
100g 00 flour + 55g egg =
1 ample serving of pasta.

Preparation and Kneading: 15 to
20 minutes
Resting: 30 minutes (For beginners,
hand rolling pasta with a mattarello,
allow 45 to 60 minutes.)
Make Ahead: The dough can be prepared a couple hours before rolling
and shaping. Cover well with plastic
wrap and keep at room temperature.
If the dough will be out for more than
an hour or if it's a hot day, keep it in
the fridge. Bring to room temperature before rolling it out.

—

Basic Egg Dough

**Makes 4 servings
(about 1 pound dough)**

2¼ cups / 300g tipo 00 flour
(see "Measure Your Flour," page 8),
plus more for dusting

3 large eggs, at room temperature

1½ teaspoons extra-virgin olive oil

1 pinch kosher or fine sea salt

Water, as needed

Large-Batch Egg Dough

**Makes 4 to 6 servings
(about 1½ pounds dough)**

3 cups / 400g tipo 00 flour (see
"Measure Your Flour," page 8),
plus more for dusting

4 large eggs, at room temperature

2 teaspoons extra-virgin olive oil

1 pinch kosher or fine sea salt

Water, as needed

The Basic Egg Dough and Large-Batch Egg Dough have the same method but yield different amounts. Don't worry, I'll tell you when to use each. As I created the recipes, I sometimes found that the large-batch formula yielded too much pasta for four people. Can there be such a thing? But, when pasta is served with a hearty sauce, veg-heavy topping, or protein, I have found that having a bit less dough is better.

1   *To bring the dough together using a machine:* In a stand mixer fitted with the paddle attachment, on low speed, combine the flour, eggs, olive oil, and salt and mix until crumbly. If using a food processor, pulse together the flour, eggs, olive oil, and salt until the dough starts coming together. Incrementally, add 1 teaspoon water at a time until the dough becomes a craggy ball and there are barely any dry crumbs of flour remaining. (Some days, it's 3 teaspoons; other days, it's a little more. Just don't add too much water, since the flour will continue to hydrate as the dough is kneaded by hand.)

To bring the dough together by hand: Place the flour in the center of a clean, dry, large, wooden work surface. Make a well with high walls, leaving some flour on the floor of the well. Add the eggs, olive oil, and salt to the well, then, using a fork and without bringing in any flour, gently beat the eggs and oil together until combined. Gradually start incorporating the flour from the inner walls into the egg mixture, whisking away any lumps as you work. Think of it as gradually making a smooth batter. When the dough starts to come together in a scraggly pile and the eggs aren't runny anymore, use a bench scraper to fold the dough onto itself a few times, then use your hands to bring the dough into a mass. (You will most likely *not* need all the flour. However, if you did incorporate it all and the dough has become dry, add 1 teaspoon water at a time until you can bring it together into a ball.) Use the bench scraper to completely clean your work surface of any drying bits of dough. Wash and dry your hands before kneading.

TIPS

Clear the decks, you'll need space!

If you're in a pinch and can't get tipo 00 flour, you can use all-purpose flour with a 9 to 11 percent protein; it just won't be as luxurious.

If making dough by hand and the eggs leak from the flour well, grab a bench scraper and scoop them back into the center of the well pronto, then try to repair the broken wall. (Think of this as a rite of passage.)

If you leave the ball of dough out in the fridge overnight, it will oxidize; but don't worry, it will return to its former color as you roll it out.

Once you've cut or shaped your pasta, it can be cooked immediately, but it's perfectly okay if it dries out.

Once your pasta is cut into the desired shape, spread it out (in a single layer) on a flour-dusted baking sheet before cooking so it doesn't stick together.

When I can, I use Happy Egg Co. organic free-range or heritage-breed eggs that have deep-amber yolks with a rich, creamy flavor.

Continued

2   Lightly flour a work surface, place the dough on the surface, and knead (see page 4) until it becomes a smooth and supple ball and springs back when lightly pressed, about 10 minutes. Remove the crease line in the dough by pinching the crease together and pushing it down with your palm.

3   Cover the ball of dough with plastic wrap, or turn a mixing bowl upside down and place it over the dough on the work surface, and let rest on the counter for 30 to 45 minutes. After resting, the dough may be sticky; if so, dust it with a little flour.

4   *If rolling pasta by machine:* Divide the dough into four equal pieces. (If using a hand-cranked pasta roller, it is easier to work by dividing into six pieces.) Work with one piece at a time, keeping the remaining dough well covered in plastic wrap. Flatten the piece of dough between your palms before feeding it through the pasta machine once on the widest setting (#1). Still on the widest setting and at low speed, feed the dough through the pasta roller, then laminate it by folding it in thirds, just as you would fold a letter to fit into an envelope. Repeat this step a handful of times, turning the dough 90 degrees between each pass. Keep your folds tidy in order to create an even rectangular sheet. Now, feed the sheet of dough through the rollers, turning the knob down incrementally to a narrower setting between each pass (there's no need to fold between passes anymore), until it's rolled to the desired thickness. If the dough feels sticky or puckers as it's rolled, sprinkle it lightly with flour and use your hand to spread it gently across the sheet before feeding it through the machine again. This helps to keep the dough flat and smooth and prevents it from getting stuck.

If rolling pasta by hand: See page 4.

5   See pages 31 to 34 for flat, shaped, and filled egg dough instructions.

6   Once the pasta is cut or filled, place on a flour-dusted baking sheet. Lightly dust a little more flour on top of the pasta so it doesn't stick. (It's perfectly okay if the pasta dries out at this stage.) If cooking within a couple of hours, simply leave on the counter. You can place stuffed pasta, uncovered, in the refrigerator for a few hours but be very careful that they don't become a sticky mess. To store stuffed or cut pasta, freeze in a single layer on a baking sheet, transfer the frozen pasta to a ziplock bag or airtight container, and freeze for about 1 month. For longer pasta, like fettuccine, make small individual portioned nests before freezing.

Continued

VARIATIONS

Saffron Egg Dough

Soak 2 teaspoons saffron threads in 1 tablespoon hot water for 20 minutes. The strands won't completely dissolve in this short time, but they look lovely when rolled into the dough. Add the saffron water, with strands, to the eggs.

Spinach Egg Dough

Steam 7 ounces fresh baby spinach until wilted, 4 to 5 minutes. Let cool completely and then squeeze out *all* the excess liquid with a clean dish towel. Finely chop or puree and then blend with the eggs before adding to the flour well.

Squid or Cuttlefish Ink Egg Dough

Add 2 to 3 tablespoons squid or cuttlefish ink to the eggs before adding them to the flour well.

White Pepper Egg Dough

Add 2 teaspoons *finely* ground white pepper to the flour. (If the pepper is too coarse, it will tear the dough when it's being rolled out.)

Flour and Gluten-Free Blends

You can vary the flavor, texture, and hue of basic egg doughs by blending flours. Since some flours are more absorbent than others, you might need to adjust the amount of fat (egg) or water added to bring the dough together. I often add an additional yolk or two when using higher-protein, sturdier flours. For gluten-free pasta, I've found Caputo Gluten Free Flour to be the simplest substitution in terms of flavor and mouthfeel.

Try blending tipo 00 flour in a 1:1 ratio with other flours such as spelt or whole wheat. For example, 1½ cups / 200g tipo 00 flour plus 1½ cups / 200g spelt flour.

For flours with more oomph, like buckwheat and dark rye, use one part alternative flour to three parts tipo 00 flour. For example, ¾ cup / 100g buckwheat flour plus 2¼ cups / 300g tipo 00 flour.

For gluten-free egg dough, substitute the same amount of Caputo Gluten-Free Flour (see page 236) for the tipo 00 flour. Knead the dough just enough to bring into a smooth ball. Instead of laminating the dough by feeding it through the pasta machine on the first setting a handful of times (since it will likely break or tear), divide the dough into four to six equal pieces. Working with one piece at a time, flatten the dough between your palms and then, on a lightly floured surface, using a rolling pin or bottle, roll out the dough until it is thin enough to be easily fed through the machine on the widest setting. Feed it through the machine, starting at #1 and working your way down through the settings to about #6. (This dough will not roll as thin as pasta with gluten.) Trim off any jagged edges from the resulting sheets.

Gnocchi

Gnocchi are so simple to make and satisfying to eat. I prefer to cut my gnocchi on the smaller size, since they will expand when cooking in the boiling water. It also helps to avoid any lurking uncooked flour.

To cook gnocchi, bring a large wide pot of lightly salted water to a boil. Add half the gnocchi and cook for 2 to 3 minutes. When they float to the surface, it's a good indication they're done. Pop one in your mouth to make sure it's cooked through. Use a large spider or slotted spoon to remove, and either finish in your chosen sauce or fry them in butter and olive oil. Cook the remaining half of the gnocchi in the same way.

Ricotta Gnocchi

Makes 4 servings
Preparation: 25 to 30 minutes
Resting: Not needed

—

1 pound whole-milk ricotta

2 large eggs

1 cup finely grated
Parmigiano-Reggiano

1 teaspoon kosher salt

1 teaspoon freshly ground
black pepper

¼ teaspoon ground white pepper

1⅓ cups / 180g all-purpose flour
or tipo 00 flour (see "Measure
Your Flour," page 8), plus more
for dusting

—

TIPS

A bench scraper is very handy for
gently lifting the gnocchi and transferring them to the boiling water.

To make this gluten-free, use Caputo's
Gluten-Free Flour (see page 236)
instead of all-purpose flour.

Delicate in nature and mild in flavor, ricotta gnocchi are attracted to simple everyday sauces. You won't need any equipment. The dough is very sticky but will come together when sprinkled with a little flour and rolled out on a well-floured wooden cutting board. This is a great pasta for beginners!

1   In a large bowl, combine the ricotta, eggs, Parmigiano, salt, black pepper, and white pepper. Gradually stir in the flour to form a dough.

2   Dust a large baking sheet with flour. Lightly flour a large wooden cutting board. Using your hands, scoop out an egg-size amount of the dough and roll it into a ball between your palms. (It will be quite sticky; that's okay. Rolling it on a floured wooden surface will help bind it all together.) Place the ball onto the floured surface and gently roll the dough into a ¾-inch-thick snake. Using a sharp knife, cut the snake into 1-inch gnocchi pieces. Using a bench scraper, lift the gnocchi onto the prepared baking sheet. Don't stack or overcrowd them or they will stick together. Repeat with the remaining dough.

3   If cooking within a couple of hours, leave the baking sheet on the counter. To store, freeze in a single layer on the baking sheet, transfer the frozen pasta to a ziplock bag or airtight container, and freeze for about 1 month. To cook, don't defrost, just boil frozen; otherwise, they will fall apart.

VARIATION

Herbed Ricotta Gnocchi

Add a handful of finely chopped soft herbs, such as chives, parsley, or marjoram, to the ricotta mixture prior to adding the flour.

Potato Gnocchi

Makes 4 servings
Preparation: 1 hour 45 minutes
Resting: Not needed

—

1½ pounds unpeeled
russet potatoes

1 large egg, beaten

⅓ cup finely grated
Pecorino Romano

½ teaspoon kosher salt

½ teaspoon ground white pepper

1½ cups / 195g all-purpose flour
or tipo 00 flour (see "Measure
Your Flour," page 8), plus more
as needed

—

TIPS

Cook the potatoes whole, in their
skins, so they don't absorb too
much water.

If you have leftover mashed potatoes, make gnocchi! I'll often make
extra mash and use it the following
evening to make gnocchi.

A bench scraper is very handy for
gently lifting the gnocchi and transferring them to the boiling water.

To make this gluten-free, use Caputo's
Gluten-Free Flour (see page 236)
instead of all-purpose flour.

Homemade potato gnocchi are divine and a completely different species to the packaged stuff. They are lighter and have a sublime, smooth, melt-in-your-mouth texture. To get this consistency, pass the boiled potatoes through a ricer, or grate on the finest side of a box grater or with a large Microplane. Potato gnocchi are sturdier than delicate ricotta gnocchi, so they can handle a hearty sauce. Use a fork or gnocchi board to create ridges that will help catch the sauce and add a little bit of panache.

1 In a large wide pot, add the potatoes and enough water to cover them (you'll also cook the gnocchi in this pot). Bring to a boil and cook until a sharp knife poked into a potato meets only a little resis-tance, 35 to 40 minutes. Turn off the heat. Remove the potatoes from the water and, when cool enough to handle, remove the skins.

2 Using a ricer, box grater, or Microplane, pass or grate the potatoes into a fine consistency, making sure there are no lumps. Spread the potatoes out on a baking sheet to dry out and cool a little.

3 In a large bowl, combine the potatoes, egg, pecorino, salt, and pepper. Gradually add the flour and use your hands to combine everything and bring the dough together.

4 Place the dough on a clean, dry, lightly floured work surface and knead just until the dough comes together in a smooth ball. If the dough feels a little sticky, add a bit more flour. If you won't be rolling out immediately, cover with a piece of plastic wrap.

5 Dust a large baking sheet with flour. Lightly flour a large wooden cutting board or work surface. Take a small piece of dough and roll it into a snake about ¾ inch thick. Using a sharp knife, cut the snake into pieces about a thumb's width. (If you'd like to give your gnocchi a little flair, roll the cut pieces along the tines of a gnocchi paddle or a fork.) Place the gnocchi on the prepared baking sheet. Repeat the process with the remaining dough.

6 If cooking within a couple of hours, leave the baking sheet on the counter. To store, freeze in a single layer of gnocchi on the baking sheet, transfer the frozen pasta to a ziplock bag or airtight con-tainer, and freeze for about 1 month. To cook, don't defrost, just boil frozen; otherwise, they will fall apart.

Semolina Dough

Now let's get into the pasta from the south of Italy. This is a dough that wants you to do everything the old-fashioned way—by hand. Semolina is made from durum wheat, and when mixed with water it makes a toothsome, rustic pasta. You don't need any special equipment—just your hands, a butter knife, and a wooden surface—to roll out and shape the dough (this helps create pasta full of texture for the sauce to cling to).

Simple Semolina Dough

Makes 4 servings

Preparation: 10 minutes
Resting: Not needed
Make Ahead: The dough can be prepared a couple of hours before rolling and shaping. Cover well with plastic wrap at room temperature.

—

2 cups semolina flour / 300g, or as needed

½ teaspoon kosher salt

¾ cup tepid water, or as needed

—

TIPS

This toothsome dough works best with smaller shapes and sizes. If the pieces are too large or thick, they will be dense, heavy, and chewy. Make sure the pieces are sized similarly so they cook evenly.

The water for making the dough should be body temperature—not cold or hot. The amount of water depends on the mill of the flour and the humidity. When in doubt, add water incrementally. If the dough feels dry when kneading and rolling, spritz it with water, or wet your hands to hydrate the dough.

Kneading the dough for about 5 minutes creates the perfect elasticity while protecting it from becoming chewy. If you knead semolina dough for only 5 minutes, you don't have to wait for it to rest and can begin shaping immediately. If you knead it for longer, it will have to rest, since you don't want it to be too chewy.

Basically, this dough is the homemade version of store-bought dried pasta that's been put through an extruder, then air-dried. I don't have an extruder at home, and I'm guessing you don't either, so I'm just going to teach you how to hand-roll orecchiette, cavatelli, and pici from this dough. You can also form other shapes full of character and charm. Stick with Italian brands of semolina flour, like Caputo's Semola di Grano Duro, Mulino Marino, and De Cecco Semola, which all have a very fine mill and feel only slightly more textured than tipo 00 flour. Don't buy coarse semolina, which is more appropriate for pizza making, not pasta. The dough comes together quickly but, for the beginner, it takes time to shape every piece of pasta. Like everything, speed and efficiency will come with practice. Be patient with yourself.

1   In a large bowl, combine the flour and salt and then gradually pour in the all the water and mix with your hands, until the mixture forms a craggy ball. If needed, incrementally add more water 1 teaspoon at a time until there are no dry crumbs of flour remaining.

2   Place the ball of dough on a large, lightly floured wooden cutting board or dry work surface. Knead the dough for about 5 minutes until smooth and springy. If the dough feels wet and sticky, add a little more flour to your work surface. If it feels dry, add a little more water. Cover the ball in plastic wrap, or turn a mixing bowl upside down and place it over the dough on the work surface, while you make your shapes or if you're not using immediately. (See pages 46 to 50 for shaping semolina dough.) Once the dough is made into the desired shapes, place the pieces in a single layer on flour-dusted baking sheets. (It's perfectly okay if the pasta dries out at this stage.)

3   If cooking within a couple of hours, leave the baking sheet on the counter. To store, freeze in a single layer on the baking sheet, transfer the frozen pasta to a ziplock bag or airtight container, and freeze for about 1 month. To cook, don't defrost, just boil frozen.

The Pasta Playground

There are myriad ways to cut and shape pasta dough. I've chosen to focus on just a few. For basic flat noodles, use a sharp knife or pasta cutter and cut one sheet at a time. As you become more experienced, you can layer sheets of floured pasta on top of one another and cut noodles without having them stick to each other. To make easy and fast work of it, use a pasta-machine cutter attachment. (I LOVE my KitchenAid pasta roller and cutter attachment.) Always work on a dry, lightly floured wooden cutting board. Dust two large baking sheets with flour to place cut and shaped pastas on. For long cut pasta, you can use a pasta drying rack or any food-safe jerry-rigged contraption (clean clothes rack, the back of a chair) on which to drape the pasta. Freshly cut or shaped pasta can be cooked immediately, but it's perfectly okay if it dries out before it's cooked.

Flat Egg Dough Pasta

Use the table at right as a guide for achieving the desired width for flat egg dough pasta—but by all means, follow your preferences. If you love heartier, chewier pasta, roll out your dough to #5 or #6. If you want a delicate, finer mouthfeel, roll out your dough thinly to #7 or #8. Remember, all fresh pasta will expand in the water, and it cooks in 2 to 3 minutes, so have your sauce ready.

LINGUINE	FETTUCCINE	TAGLIATELLE
(⅛ inch wide): Roll out dough to #3	(¼ inch wide): Roll out dough to #4 or #5	(⅜ inch wide): Roll out dough to #5
PAPPARDELLE	CANNELLONI	LASAGNA
(1 inch wide): Roll out dough to #6	Roll out dough to #7	Roll out dough to #8

Shaped Egg Dough Pasta

To get you started, here are some of the shapes that I make most often. The dough should be hydrated enough to shape and seal the pasta easily. If the dough dries out, dab it with a little water to help seal the pasta shapes.

FARFALLE

(butterflies or bow ties)

Roll out dough to #5 or #6

(Pictured) These petite butterflies are made from small rectangular pieces of pasta. Using a sharp knife or pasta cutter, cut three 1½-inch strips across the entire sheet of pasta. Then, using a fluted cutter, cut these strips every 3 inches so that you make small rectangles. Working one at a time, using your index finger and thumb, squeeze the center of the rectangle together to form the bow-tie shape, then firmly press where the layers overlap to ensure uniform thickness and that it holds together. Dab a little water at the center of the rectangle, if needed, to make the pasta stick. Let them dry out a little before cooking so they hold their shape.

GARGANELLI

(an elegant penne)

Roll out dough to #6

(Pictured) Using a sharp knife, cut the sheet of pasta into 1½-inch squares. Lay one square diagonally on a gnocchi board, if you would like decorative lines. Place a small, pencil-size wooden dowel at the corner closest to you and roll the pasta around it, until you get to the opposite corner. Press down to secure, then slide the dough off the dowel. If the tips unroll, dab them with a little water and use the pressure of your finger to seal.

MALTAGLIATI

(irregularly shaped pieces)

Roll out dough to #6, #7, or #8

Maltagliati means "badly cut" in Italian. This is a good one for the kids. Using a sharp knife or pasta cutter, cut pieces of a similar size. Think small triangles, rectangles, diamonds, and more. Unleash your creativity.

STROZZAPRETI

(twisted hand-rolled ribbons)

Roll out dough to #6

Strozzapreti means "priest choker" in Italian. (Uplifting, right?) Using a sharp knife or pasta cutter, cut 1 by 2-inch rectangles. Place a rectangle between your palms, then gently twist and roll the dough between your hands so that each strand is stretched into a twisted ribbon about 4 inches long.

Filled Egg Dough Pasta

Filled pastas, like all good things, take time. At first you will likely fumble, fiddle, and swear at me, but with practice, finesse will come. Start with pansotti as it's the easiest. Cut squares of dough, put a small amount of filling in the center of them, fold into triangles, and seal. Done. Next, work your way to mezzelune, round (pictured), or square ravioli. Then tackle tortellini or agnolotti when you have a handle on filled pastas. As you gain experience, you'll likely roll your dough thinner; this is preferable for filled pastas. Don't throw out any of the dough trimmings, these maltagliati (see page 32) can be cooked and fed to any hungry, impatient souls. Invite your friends over and make an afternoon of it. That way you can offer each other moral support.

IDEAS FOR FILLINGS & COMBINATIONS

Think seasonally and get creative with flavor combinations you love. The possibilities are endless. I could have written a book just on filled pastas! Ideally, the fillings should have a smooth mouthfeel that won't compete with the pasta's texture nor puncture it. Most of the time, you'll want to finely chop, sauté, puree, or do a combination of all three to prepare the filling. Avoid using raw ingredients that won't fully cook in less than 4 minutes, the time it takes to cook the pasta. Filled pastas are a great way to repurpose leftovers and use up tired produce.

You'll need about 2½ cups of filling for every recipe of Large-Batch Egg Dough (page 16). Here are some combination suggestions for filled pastas to get your creative juices flowing, once you master the shapes:

Bacala, sunchokes, and olives	Mushroom, leeks, and crème fraîche	Peas, ricotta, Meyer lemon, and Serrano ham
Ricotta, spinach, and nutmeg	Taleggio cheese, walnuts, and mascarpone	White bean, garlic, and prosciutto

Also see page 236 for some helpful tools to use when filling pasta.

Tips for Filling Pasta

- Both the dough and the filling can be made in advance.

- If you're using a hand-cranked pasta roller or are a newbie to making filled pastas, try dividing your dough into six (rather than four) pieces in order to work with slightly smaller sheets.

- Dry dough is very hard to shape and seal, so work with one sheet of dough at a time and keep any dough you're not working with well covered with plastic wrap. Once the pastas are filled, they can be left uncovered. Similarly, a dough that is too wet can also be difficult to work with.

- Beginners should roll the dough down to #5 or #6, since it will be easier to work with.

- If the dough is too dry, a spray bottle of water is invaluable. A light misting will keep the dough hydrated without making it too wet. It also makes shaping, filling, and sealing filled pastas easier. *Before* placing the filling on the dough, lightly spritz the whole sheet of dough from above. Conversely, if the dough is really sticky once it's rolled out, let it dry out a little.

- Hot fillings can melt uncooked dough. Don't worry if some filling smooshes out a little; just wipe it off. Similarly, wet fillings can seep through the dough and make your pasta stick to the surface below and rip it open.

- Overstuffing filled pastas makes shaping and sealing challenging and may result in bursting during cooking. Think teaspoons, not tablespoons. Also think about the flavors in the filling. Are they strong? If so, keep the filling amount small. For subtle flavors, you could use a little more stuffing.

- I often use a small round cookie cutter that fits snugly just around the filling to shape the filling and help push out the air that may be trapped. But be careful not to cut through the dough.

- Use your fingers to push out any air around the filling or in between the layers of dough before sealing the filled pasta. Air pockets can cause filled pastas to burst or fill with water as they cook.

- Seal the filled pasta by using your fingers to gently press the layers of dough together, so they become the thickness of a single layer. A ravioli cutter also helps to seal and cut filled pasta. If you don't own a ravioli cutter, use the tines of a fork to add a decorative edge and seal the layers.

- Place the filled pasta on a parchment-lined or flour-dusted baking sheet until ready to cook. Make sure they are not touching each other, so they don't stick together.

- Take any moist, leftover bits of dough, roll them into a ball and slightly flatten, then feed through the machine again. These pieces are your maltagliati (see page 32).

- Don't put uncooked filled pastas, even if covered, in the refrigerator or they'll turn into a soft, sticky mess. It's fine to leave filled pastas uncovered, sitting out at room temperature while you're working. If not cooking soon, freeze the filled pastas on baking sheets, then transfer them into airtight containers. Never thaw frozen pastas; always cook them straight from the freezer.

- Filling long sheets of dough takes experience, so feel free to cut your sheet of dough into equally sized, smaller rectangles that are more manageable.

Shapes for Filled Egg-Dough Pasta

To make sure you don't end up hating me and saying, "simple, my ass," I've kept most of the filled pasta to the basic shapes we can all wrap our heads around. Beginners might want to work their way up to agnolotti and tortellini. Traditional tortellini have just 1 gram of pasta and 1 gram of filling. Dainty tortellini such as these take a bit of experience, dexterity, and speed, so it's okay to start with slightly larger squares of dough as directed.

AGNOLOTTI

This is going to be a challenge. At first, you might not be able to get two rows of filled agnolotti from one rolled sheet of dough. If you can't pull it off, don't worry. Just follow along making one row per sheet, like in the photos, and use the rest of the sheet for Maltagliati (page 32). But let's give it a shot.

Divide the dough into four pieces. Roll one piece through the pasta machine down to #5 or #6, aiming to have the sheet as wide as possible. Keep the other pieces covered in plastic wrap as you work. Lay out the sheet on a floured surface. Trim off the ragged ends. If the dough feels too sticky, just give it a moment to dry out a little so it's easier to work with. Cut the sheet in half lengthwise, then cut in half down the center, so you have four equal-size rectangles. (I've found dividing the sheet like this makes forming agnolotti more manageable. As you get more experienced you might not need to do this.) Working with one rectangle at a time, spoon about ½ teaspoon of filling, 1 inch apart along the length of the rectangle, and ½ inch up from the bottom edge. Carefully lift the bottom edge of the pasta and drape it over the filling to enclose it, leaving ¼ inch of the bottom sheet exposed, like a seam. Seal the edge where the two layers of pasta meet. Using your pointer finger and thumb, pinch between each mound of filling, and at the same time, rock the filled sheet away from you, so it's sitting up on itself. With the filled rectangle in this position, use a fluted cutter to cut away from you on either side of the filling, separating each agnolotti. This action creates the trademark agnolotti shelf that collects the sauce. Transfer the agnolotti to a flour-dusted baking sheet. Repeat this process with the remaining rectangles, and the rest of the dough. Phew!

PANSOTTI

Pansotti means "pot-bellied" in Italian. Divide the dough into four pieces. Roll one piece through the pasta machine to #6. Keep the other pieces covered in plastic wrap as you work. Lay out the sheet on a floured surface and cut it into approximately 2-inch squares. Pipe or place about ½ teaspoon of filling in the center of each square. Using a finger dipped in water, *lightly* moisten the perimeter. Fold the square in half diagonally, enclosing the filling to form a triangle. Using your fingers, push out any air and help shape the mound of filling into a neat triangle. Seal well and then transfer the pansotti to a flour-dusted baking sheet and repeat with the remaining dough.

RAVIOLI

Ravioli can be made into a variety of shapes and sizes. These options are the easiest.

Mezzelune Ravioli

(Pictured) *Mezzelune* means "half-moon" in Italian. Divide the dough into four pieces. Roll one piece through the pasta machine to #6. Keep the other pieces covered in plastic wrap as you work. Lay out the sheet on a floured surface and use a round cookie cutter (about 3 inches in diameter) to cut out as many circles as possible. Pipe or place 1 teaspoon of filling in the center of each circle. Using a finger dipped in water, *lightly* moisten the perimeter. Fold the circle in half to make a half-moon shape. Using your fingers, push out any air and help shape the mound of filling and then seal well. Using the tines of a fork, decorate the edges, if desired. Transfer the mezzelune to a flour-dusted baking sheet and repeat with the remaining dough.

Round or Square Ravioli

Divide the dough into four pieces. Roll one piece through the pasta machine to #6. Keep the other pieces covered in plastic wrap as you work. Cut the sheet in half so you have two matching rectangles. Lay out both sheets on a floured surface.

For round ravioli: Using either a round ravioli stamp or a cookie cutter, *lightly* imprint as many circles as you can fit on one sheet. This will help guide you on where to place the filling. (Be careful not to cut through the pasta!) Pipe or place a teaspoon or so of filling in the center of each circle.

For square ravioli: On one of the sheets, pipe or place single teaspoons of filling, about two or three finger widths apart, in two uniform rows along the sheet, making sure to leave about ½ inch around the edges of the dough.

Using a finger dipped in water, *lightly* moisten the dough around each mound of filling. Carefully place the other sheet of dough directly on top of the first. Using your fingers, push out the air trapped between the dough layers, then seal the layers together. Using a ravioli cutter, cookie cutter, or sharp knife, cut out each ravioli. Pick them up and use your fingers to make sure the layers are well sealed. Transfer the ravioli to a flour-dusted baking sheet and repeat with the remaining dough.

TORTELLINI

Divide the dough into four pieces. Roll one piece through the pasta machine to #6. Keep the other pieces covered in plastic wrap as you work. Lay out the sheet on a floured surface and cut it into approximately 2-inch squares. Pipe or place ½ teaspoon of filling in the center of each square. Using a finger dipped in water, *lightly* moisten the dough around the perimeter. Fold the square in half diagonally, enclosing the filling and forming a triangle. Using your fingers, push out any air between the layers of dough and the filling, then seal well. Pinch the bottom two corners of the triangle to flatten and slightly elongate the dough, then wrap them around your pointer finger like a ring until the tips overlap. Press the dough together into a single thickness and seal well. Transfer the tortellini to a flour-dusted baking sheet and repeat with the remaining dough.

Laminating Dough with Herbs & Flowers: Peter Rabbit Pasta

1 recipe Basic Egg Dough (page 16) or Large-Batch Egg Dough (page 16), made through Step 2

1 to 2 cups small soft herbs and/or edible flowers

This pasta is pure joy, the Liberty London fabric of pasta. You'll be stunned by the beauty of herb-laminated pasta and how easy it is to make. There's something mesmerizing about watching petite soft herbs and petals—basil, marjoram, chervil, flat-leaf parsley, carrot-top greens, nasturtiums, and other edible flowers—transform and elongate when they're rolled between layers of egg dough. The ochre colors of nasturtium petals even bleed a little into the dough, creating a painterly effect. Decoratively laminated dough is best showcased in filled pastas or wider-cut fettuccine and pappardelle. A little rabbit in a blue jacket would be besotted. And so will you.

1   While the dough is resting, gently pull off the petals and leaves from the herbs or flowers and discard the stems. Cover with a damp paper towel to keep them fresh while you roll your dough. Divide the dough into four equal pieces.

2   Working with one piece at a time, roll the dough to setting #6 or #7, keeping the rest covered in plastic wrap. Place the sheet of dough on a lightly floured work surface. On one-half of the sheet, place one-fourth of the soft herbs or petals. (Make sure to leave space between the pieces as well as along the edges, since they will stretch out.) Using your fingers, brush a bit of water on the leaves or petals if they're not sticking to the pasta and then moisten the perimeter of the pasta sheet. Bring the remaining blank half of the dough over onto the herb-filled half, as if you were closing a book. Starting at the fold, lightly press the dough together, like pressing flowers in a book. Carefully lift and guide the sheet through the machine, starting at setting #4 and working your way down to setting #6 or #7. If you're making filled pasta, it's now time to fill, cut, and shape this first sheet before it dries out. If you're making pappardelle or fettuccine, roll the remaining pieces of dough, then cut the sheets into the desired width.

Shaped Semolina Dough Pasta

You don't need special equipment to make shaped semolina pasta; a wooden skewer, a box grater, a Microplane, a butter knife, or just your fingers stretching and shaping the eggless dough. A wooden surface can create an interesting plate of pasta, full of texture for the sauce to cling to. To not overwhelm you, I'll teach you these three ride-or-die semolina classics.

CAVATELLI

Cavatelli translates to "little hollows." This is very similar to making gnocchi. Take a small piece of the dough and keep the remaining dough covered in plastic wrap. On a large, lightly floured wooden board, roll the dough into a long snake about ½ inch in diameter. Cut the snake into pieces about two-fingers wide. Working with one piece at a time, roll on a lightly floured wooden surface or gnocchi board. Place the tips of your index and middle fingers on the very outer edge of the dough and firmly press down, pulling and rolling the dough toward you. This motion stretches, flattens, and creates the textured curl of cavatelli that will hold the sauce. With experience, you might be able to use both hands at once to roll and shape. Lay the finished cavatelli on a flour-dusted baking sheet and repeat with the remaining dough.

For Christmas, I bought myself a vintage BeeBo cavatelli maker on eBay. It's a compact, metal, hand-cranked machine that attaches to the kitchen counter. You feed rolls of dough through two small rollers that shape and spit out cut cavatelli. It oozes charm and nostalgia. My son, Ned, is into it.

ORECCHIETTE

Orecchiette translates to "little ears." Take a small piece of the dough and keep the remaining dough covered in plastic wrap. On a large, lightly floured wooden board, roll the dough into a long snake about ½ inch in diameter. Cut the dough snake into ½-inch pieces. Working with one piece at a time, place a butter knife or the side of your thumb on the far edge of the dough and drag it, flattening the dough across the board toward you. You'll get a feel for the correct pressure. Gently pick up the pasta and place it on the tip of your thumb, then invert and roll it back over your thumb like a cap. Lay the finished orecchiette on a flour-dusted baking sheet and repeat with the remaining dough.

PICI

Cut a small piece of the dough, about the size of an apricot and keep the remaining dough covered in plastic wrap. On a large, lightly floured wooden board, roll the dough into a long ribbon. Start with your hands in the center and apply even pressure, while pushing out, until you have a long smooth noodle that's a little thinner than an udon noodle, 1/8 to 1/4 inch. If the noodle gets too long, cut it in half and work the two parts separately. There's no rule as to how long your pici should be; they can be long or short, like trofie. Lay the finished pici on a flour-dusted baking sheet and repeat with the remaining dough.

Everyday Sauces & Crunchy Bits

Tomato-based sauces and pestos are what I fall back on again and again when making pasta. It's impossible to tire of them, and they require little bandwidth. In fact, these recipes are so simple that you'll likely commit your favorites to memory.

Tomato Sauces

Here is a range of red sauces from light Nonna's Homemade Passata to medium-bodied Mama Sordo's Red Sauce to full-bodied Luxurious Pomodoro in a Flash. If I don't have passata on hand, I use canned San Marzano crushed tomatoes. And sometimes I cheat even more and use a bottle of Rao's marinara sauce. It's all good.

Nonna's Homemade Passata

Makes approximately 1 quart

—

5 pounds ridiculously ripe Roma or Early Girl tomatoes, halved

2 large yellow onions, quartered

6 garlic cloves

½ cup extra-virgin olive oil

1 teaspoon kosher salt

1 teaspoon freshly ground black pepper

1 bunch basil leaves

—

TIP

You can use this passata wherever canned tomatoes are called for throughout *Simple Pasta*.

Passata is a simple, light, fruity tomato sauce. It is also the base for more complex red sauces. The definition of simple done well is homemade pasta, topped with this passata that's had a dollop or two of butter melted in, finished with fresh basil and loads of Parmigiano. The ideal time to prepare and bottle homemade passata is toward the end of summer, when tomatoes are full of flavor, inexpensive, and abundant. My friend's Italian mother and aunt make passata every year. Apparently, the day is full of shenanigans and both families come away with enough tomato sauce to get them through the winter. They hold a family record of two hundred bottles in a day. That's a lot of tomatoes! When I shared the story with my mom, she bought enough tomatoes to fill a bathtub and recruited her sister to help. So why not start a new annual tradition of bottling passata in your family or with friends? This recipe can be easily scaled up; just remember to work in batches.

1   Preheat the oven to 350°F. Line two large baking sheets with parchment paper.

2   Scatter the tomatoes, onions, and garlic across the prepared baking sheets, toss and coat everything with the olive oil, then season with the salt and pepper. Roast until the tomatoes have softened and burst, 40 to 45 minutes. Remove from the oven and let cool slightly. Set a food mill or fine-mesh strainer over a large saucepan and pass the tomatoes through the mill, separating the skins and seeds from the pulp. Discard the skins and seeds. If you'd like the passata to be thicker and have a bit more body, simmer the strained tomatoes over low heat, until the sauce reaches your desired consistency. Stir in the basil. Serve while warm, or let cool and then keep in airtight container in the refrigerator for up to 2 days.

To Can Passata for the Winter Months

If you'd like the passata to have a shelf life, heat processing is essential. There is nothing in the recipe (such as vinegar) to inhibit the growth of bacteria.

Special Equipment

A food mill, chinois or fine-mesh strainer, and glass jars with lids (such as Ball or WECK jars) are necessary. A funnel is helpful but not essential.

Sterilize the jars

Sterilizing is an essential step to remove any microorganisms that could contaminate your passata. Keep your hands off! Use tongs or a clean dish towel to handle the jars.

To sterilize using the oven method: Preheat the oven to 220°F. Wash the jars and lids in hot, soapy water and rinse well or put them through the dishwasher. Once washed, place the glass jars faceup on a baking sheet. Place the tray in the oven until the jars are completely dry, about 15 minutes. Pour boiling water over the lids carefully, then drain and air-dry.

To sterilize using the boiling method: Put the jars and lids into a large pot, cover with water, and bring to a boil for 5 minutes. Using tongs, carefully remove the jars and allow them to air-dry completely (or put them in a 220°F oven for 15 minutes).

Fill the jars

Have both jars and sauce close to the same temperature to prevent thermal shock, which can break the glass. Fill the jars with the passata but leave a small space between the sauce and the lid, since the sauce will expand during heat processing. Remove any air bubbles that may breed bacteria simply by tapping the jar. Pop in a basil leaf or two on top before sealing.

Heat process

Put an old clean dishcloth at the bottom of a very large, deep pot or multiple pots. Place the filled, sealed jars on top of the cloth, making sure they don't touch the sides of the pot. Pour water that's about the same temperature as the jars into the pot until the jars are almost submerged. Turn the heat to medium-low and maintain a steady boil for 1 hour, adding more boiling water as necessary to keep the water level almost at the top of the jars. The lids will become convex and puff up. Carefully remove the jars from the pot and leave them at room temperature overnight. The next day, the jar lids should be concave, confirming they're vacuum-sealed. If they don't seal, keep in the refrigerator and use within 2 days, gift to neighbors, or troubleshoot online. Now, get creative designing your own label and store the jars in a cool, dark pantry for 1 month.

Mama Sordo's Red Sauce

Makes approximately 3 cups

—

¼ cup extra-virgin olive oil

1 small yellow onion, finely diced

2 medium carrots, finely diced

Kosher salt

2 garlic cloves, finely diced

1 cup chicken stock or vegetable stock

One 28-ounce can San Marzano crushed tomatoes, or 3½ cups Nonna's Homemade Passata (page 55)

This is a medium-bodied, bright tomato sauce. When I was in university, I lived with Anna, a friend whose Italian Australian mother, Mama Sordo, used to come and stock our freezer with this red sauce and her homemade Bolognese. I'd start to surreptitiously eat them when Anna nonchalantly left them for weeks. As a broke student, it was like eating at a favorite trattoria. Years later, Mama kindly shared her recipe with me. It is exceptionally versatile, with a touch of sweetness from the caramelized onion-carrot base that gets blitzed in a food processor before the tomatoes are added. This extra step that Mama taught me was an epiphany; it integrates the flavors and creates a lovely consistency. (If you're short on time, skip this step; it'll still be great.) This sauce is fantastic with Cannelloni—Let's Bring It Back! (page 217) and meatballs (see page 172).

1   In a heavy-bottomed saucepan over medium-low heat, warm the olive oil. Add the onion and carrot, season with ¼ teaspoon salt, and sauté until softened, about 10 minutes. Add the garlic and sauté for 1 minute more.

2   Transfer the mixture to a food processor with a splash of the chicken stock and blend until smooth. Return the pureed mixture to the pan.

3   Add the tomatoes, remaining stock, and ½ teaspoon salt. Turn the heat to low and bring to a gentle simmer for about 10 minutes. Season with additional salt, if necessary. Serve while warm, or let cool and then keep in airtight container in the refrigerator for up to 2 days.

Luxurious Pomodoro in a Flash

Makes approximately 3 cups

—

½ cup extra-virgin olive oil

4 to 6 anchovy fillets, chopped

3 garlic cloves, finely chopped

2 tablespoons oregano leaves

One 28-ounce can San Marzano crushed tomatoes, or 3½ cups Nonna's Homemade Passata (page 55)

¼ teaspoon kosher salt

Freshly ground black pepper

MAKE THIS! You could put this sauce on pretty much any pasta and be happy. You'd think this full-bodied sauce had been simmering for hours, not just twenty minutes. Your instincts might tell you that you're putting in too much oil, but when you toss it through a pound of pasta, you'll realize the amount is just right; it helps the sauce cling to the pasta. My dear Italian American friend Amy taught me this, and she credits Marcella Hazan.

1   In a large skillet over medium-low heat, warm the olive oil.

2   Add the anchovies to the skillet and cook them slowly, mashing with a wooden spoon until they melt into the oil. (Don't let the oil get too hot or it will fry the anchovies rather than melt them.)

3   Add the garlic and oregano to the anchovies and sauté for a few minutes. (Get your face in there and take a whiff of that glorious aroma.)

4   Finally, add the tomatoes to the skillet, season with the salt and pepper, and let simmer for 20 minutes. Serve while warm, or let cool and then keep in airtight container in the refrigerator for up to 2 days.

VARIATIONS

Amatriciana

Porky and peppery! Omit the anchovies; substitute 8 ounces diced pancetta, smoked bacon, or, for the real deal, guanciale (skin removed); and sauté in the oil for 4 to 5 minutes. Omit the garlic and oregano and add ¾ teaspoon red pepper flakes. Add the tomatoes and increase the salt and black pepper to ½ teaspoon each. The fruitiness of the tomatoes will be more front and center; if they lack sweetness, add 1 teaspoon brown sugar.

Arrabiata

Arrabiata means "angry" in Italian, a nod to this sauce's spiciness. Omit the anchovies and double the amount of garlic to 6 cloves. Add 1 or 2 small seeded and finely chopped fresh red chiles and sauté with the garlic. Add 1 teaspoon brown sugar and an additional ½ teaspoon salt.

Puttanesca

Pungent and salty! Prepare the sauce through Step 3, then add ¾ cup chopped olives (black oil-cured, kalamata, or green) along with the tomatoes, salt, and pepper. Add 2 tablespoons capers and ¼ cup finely chopped flat-leaf parsley.

Pestos

Pesto is an excuse to play. In the summer, it's all about basil; in the fall, I lean toward broccoli and kale; and in winter, I often use marinated vegetables in place of herbs. Remember, the secret ingredient to make creamy pesto pasta is the addition of starchy pasta water. Use as much as needed when tossing the pesto with the pasta. Leftover pesto can be dolloped on a salad, bruschetta, or panini or served as a dip on an antipasto plate.

Classic Genovese Pesto with a Twist of Opal Basil

Makes approximately 2 cups

—

4 cups packed Genovese basil leaves

1¾ cups finely grated Parmigiano-Reggiano

¾ cup pine nuts, toasted, plus more for garnishing

3 garlic cloves

¾ cup extra-virgin olive oil, or as needed

½ teaspoon kosher salt

Freshly ground black pepper

1 handful opal basil leaves

I've tried to grow basil in my garden in San Francisco to no avail, but I'll keep trying. If I spot opal basil at the nursery, I always bring home a pot of it for my daughter Opal (who never turns down pesto). In this Genovese sauce, I use it as an accent. The dark purple leaves look fabulous scattered on top with toasted pine nuts. If you can't find opal basil, no biggie, just use petite, traditional Genovese basil leaves.

1   In a food processor, combine the Genovese basil, Parmigiano, pine nuts, and garlic and blend to make a smooth-ish paste. Scrape down the sides of the processor using a rubber spatula.

2   With the machine still running, gradually pour the olive oil into the food processor through the tube, blending until combined. Season with the salt and pepper.

3   When ready to serve, garnish the pesto with the opal basil leaves and pine nuts.

—

TIPS

Blanch the greens for about 10 seconds in boiling water, then shock them in an ice bath to keep the pesto a vivid green. Pat the greens dry with a dish towel or paper towel.

These pesto recipes use a food processor for ease, but feel free to use a mortar and pestle when working with soft herbs.

Pesto can be stored in the fridge for up to 1 week or frozen in an airtight container for up to 1 month. Make sure to cover the pesto with a thin layer of olive oil so that it doesn't oxidize. To bring stored pesto back to life, stir in a little fresh lemon juice and perhaps a splash of olive oil.

Charred Broccoli, Cashew & Pecorino Pesto

Makes approximately 2 cups

—

5 cups broccoli florets
(about 2 large heads broccoli)

1½ cups extra-virgin olive oil,
or as needed

Kosher salt

½ cup unsalted cashews, toasted

1½ cups finely grated
Pecorino Romano

2 garlic cloves

4 teaspoons lemon juice

Freshly ground black pepper

This is a rustic pesto. Use the broccoli stalks to make some crunchy chips to sprinkle on top of the dish with a smattering of red pepper flakes. First, peel the stalks with a vegetable peeler before slicing them very thinly. Then, in a cast-iron skillet or frying pan over medium heat, warm a splash of olive oil. Add the sliced stalks and fry on both sides until crisp. Lightly season with salt while still warm.

1   Preheat the oven to 400°F. Line a baking sheet with parchment paper.

2   On the prepared baking sheet, toss the broccoli florets with ¼ cup of the olive oil and then season with salt. Roast until the broccoli is tender and lightly charred, 15 to 20 minutes, turning halfway through the roasting time. Let cool slightly.

3   In a food processor, combine the broccoli, cashews, pecorino, garlic, and lemon juice and blend to make a coarse paste. Scrape down the sides of the processor with a rubber spatula.

4   With the machine still running, gradually pour the remaining 1¼ cups olive oil into the food processor through the tube, blending until combined. It will have some body. Season with salt and pepper. Serve while warm, or let cool and then keep in airtight container in the refrigerator for up to 2 days.

Cavolo Nero, Parmigiano & Pistachio Pesto

Makes approximately 2 cups

—

6 cups (about 2 small bunches) cavolo nero, stemmed

½ cup shelled, salted pistachios

1¼ cups finely grated Parmigiano-Reggiano

3 teaspoons lemon juice

2 garlic cloves

1 cup extra-virgin olive oil, or as needed

½ teaspoon kosher salt

Freshly ground black pepper

Cavolo nero (lacinato kale) is a dark-leafed wild cabbage often called Tuscan kale. Don't confuse cavolo nero with the type of sturdy kale that needs massaging; it is a delicate leaf closer to spinach. It makes a deep-emerald-green pesto that's a knockout in a winter vegetable lasagna (see page 223).

1   Bring a large pot of salted water to a boil. In a large bowl, combine equal parts water and ice cubes to prepare an ice bath.

2   Add the kale to the boiling water and blanch for 3 to 4 minutes, then, using a spider or slotted spoon, transfer to the ice bath. Drain, squeeze out all the liquid, pat dry with a dish towel, and then coarsely chop.

3   In a food processor, combine the kale, pistachios, Parmigiano, lemon juice, and garlic and blend to make a coarse paste. Scrape down the sides of the processor with a rubber spatula.

4   With the machine still running, gradually pour the olive oil into the food processor through the tube, blending until smooth and glossy. Season with the salt and pepper. Serve while warm, or let cool and then keep in airtight container in the refrigerator for up to 2 days.

Artichoke, Almond & Asiago Pesto

Makes approximately 2 cups

—

1 cup oil-marinated artichokes, drained

⅓ cup Marcona almonds or toasted almonds

1½ cups finely grated Asiago or Pecorino Romano

2 garlic cloves

Zest of 1 lemon, plus 1 tablespoon lemon juice

1 cup extra-virgin olive oil, or as needed

1½ cups flat-leaf parsley

1 teaspoon kosher salt

Freshly ground black pepper

I love this zingy pesto. Make sure you use oil-marinated artichoke hearts rather than those canned in water; it makes a difference. This pesto is wonderful as a dip, spread on a salami and mortadella sandwich, smeared on bruschetta, or tossed through any short-length pasta.

1   In a food processor, combine the artichokes, almonds, Asiago, garlic, lemon zest, and lemon juice and blend to make a coarse paste. Scrape down the sides of the processor with a rubber spatula.

2   With the machine still running, gradually pour the olive oil into the food processor through the tube, blending to combine. Finally, add the parsley and pulse until just integrated (no need to pulse it into oblivion). Season with the salt and pepper. Serve while warm, or let cool and then keep in an airtight container in the refrigerator for up to 2 days.

Nana's Nasturtium & Macadamia Pesto

Makes approximately 2 cups

—

3½ cups small nasturtium leaves and tender stems (or arugula), plus nasturtium petals for garnishing

1⅓ cups flat-leaf parsley

⅔ cup finely grated Parmigiano-Reggiano

⅔ cup macadamia nuts, toasted

2 garlic cloves

Zest of 1 lemon, plus 2 teaspoons lemon juice

⅔ cup extra-virgin olive oil

½ teaspoon kosher salt

Freshly ground black pepper

I credit my mum, who transformed nasturtiums that she grew on her Sydney balcony-garden into this macadamia nut pesto. If you plant nasturtiums, they'll run wild. The stems, leaves, flowers, and seeds are all edible, and have a slightly spicy, citrus flavor. This pesto doesn't oxidize; go figure. Serve some on pasta as a starter or on a simple ricotta-filled pasta to wake up the taste buds. Make sure to channel your inner Shakespearean Titania and scatter the nasturtium petals over the pasta.

1   In a food processor, combine the nasturtiums, parsley, Parmigiano, nuts, garlic, lemon zest, and lemon juice and blend into a coarse paste. Scrape down the sides of the processor with a rubber spatula.

2   With the machine still running, gradually pour the olive oil into the food processor through the tube, blending to combine. Season with the salt and pepper.

3   Serve while warm, garnished with the nasturtium petals, or let cool and then keep in an airtight container in the refrigerator for up to 2 days.

Walnut, Anchovy & Parsley Pesto

Makes approximately 2 cups

—

4 cups flat-leaf parsley, with tender stems

10 oil-packed anchovies

1¼ cups walnuts, toasted

2 garlic cloves

1½ cups finely grated Comté or Pecorino Toscano

1 tablespoon sherry vinegar or red wine vinegar

1¼ cups extra-virgin olive oil, or as needed

½ teaspoon kosher salt

Freshly ground black pepper

This sharp, confident combination has creamy, buttery walnuts to temper the saltiness of the anchovies. It's perfect to serve around the holidays, when walnuts are harvested.

1   In a food processor, combine the parsley, anchovies, walnuts, garlic, Comte, and vinegar and blend into a coarse paste. Scrape down the sides of the processor with a rubber spatula.

2   With the machine still running, gradually pour the olive oil into the food processor through the tube, blending to combine. Season with the salt and pepper. Serve while warm, or let cool and then keep in airtight container in the refrigerator for up to 2 days.

Crunchy Bits

Pasta loves to be topped with a smattering of crunchy bits. You can't get much better than crispy bread crumbs, but also try frying capers, or scallions; woody herbs, like sage; or guanciale, ground chorizo, or Italian sausage in a little olive oil to crisp them up. Or, make a gremolata of sorts with a combination of fresh herbs, toasted nuts, citrus zest, grated cheese, and garlic, all crushed together in a mortar and pestle with a splash of olive oil. Here are some of my tried-and-true bread crumb combos.

Basic Bread Crumbs

Makes approximately 1 cup

—

3 large slices bread,
cut into 1-inch cubes

For flavorful bread crumbs, you need to use good bread: ciabatta, sourdough, rye, walnut, or olive bread. This is the moment to round up all the stale ends that have been hanging around. If cooked in oil or butter, store in an airtight container in the refrigerator for a couple of days and rewarm with a splash more oil or a smattering of fresh herbs just before serving.

1   Preheat the oven to 300°F. Toast the bread cubes for 10 to 15 minutes to further dry them out. Transfer to a food processor and pulse into fine crumbs. Having a few motley-sized ones provides a welcomed character.

2   Transfer to an airtight container and store at room temperature for a couple of weeks, or in the freezer for a couple of months.

VARIATIONS

Garlic Butter & Chile Bread Crumbs

In a skillet over medium heat, sauté 1 cup bread crumbs with 4 tablespoons unsalted butter and 2 grated garlic cloves, stirring often until golden brown, 2 to 3 minutes. Stir in ¼ teaspoon crushed red pepper flakes and season with salt and pepper.

Guanciale & Ciabatta Bread Crumbs

In a skillet over medium heat, sauté 1 cup ciabatta bread crumbs in the rendered fat from 4 ounces guanciale, pancetta, or bacon, stirring often until golden brown, 2 to 3 minutes. Season with salt and pepper.

Sourdough, Herb & Parmigiano Bread Crumbs

In a skillet over medium heat, sauté 1 cup sourdough bread crumbs with 3 tablespoons extra-virgin olive oil, stirring often until golden brown, 2 to 3 minutes. Stir in ¼ cup finely chopped fresh herbs, like parsley, marjoram, oregano, or a combination, and 3 tablespoons finely grated Parmigiano and season with salt and pepper.

Walnut & Anchovy Bread Crumbs

In a skillet over medium heat, melt 3 chopped anchovy fillets in ¼ cup extra-virgin olive oil. Add ¼ cup chopped walnuts and sauté for 1 minute before adding ¾ cup bread crumbs, ¼ cup coarsely chopped flat-leaf parsley, and 1 teaspoon lemon zest. Continue to sauté, stirring often until golden brown, 2 to 3 minutes. Season with salt and pepper.

"GB in the House" Garlic Bread

Makes 4 servings

—

One 8-ounce crusty sourdough baguette, halved lengthwise

8 tablespoons salted butter, melted

4 garlic cloves, finely grated

½ cup finely chopped flat-leaf parsley

2 to 4 tablespoons finely grated Parmigiano-Reggiano

¼ teaspoon kosher salt

Freshly ground black pepper

How could I not include a garlic bread recipe in *Simple Pasta*? Often, I'll melt a couple of anchovies into the butter for a full-bodied experience. Back in my waitressing days at an Italian restaurant, *GB* was the shorthand for garlic bread, and it was scrawled at the top of nearly every order sent to the kitchen. Everyone loves it.

1   Preheat the oven to 350°F. Line a baking sheet with aluminum foil. Place the bread on the baking sheet, cut-side up.

2   In a small bowl, combine the melted butter, garlic, and parsley and stir to incorporate. Spoon or brush the butter mixture over the bread, sprinkle the Parmigiano on top, and season with the salt and pepper.

3   Bake for 5 minutes, then place under the broiler for 3 minutes more, or until golden. Tear into it!

Spring

Crack the windows, find that sunny spot in the kitchen, and try making a new pasta shape. Pat yourself on the back and then coat that pasta in butter. Or even better, try the schmaltz of a roast chicken. Pick up sugar snap or English peas, artichokes, asparagus, any alliums, and nettles that all go well with pasta (and chicken). Try scattering edible petals or soft herbs in between two sheets of egg dough (see page 45). It's just like pressing flowers, and it's good for your spirits. Then make the loveliest ricotta ravioli that you sure can't buy. For cooler nights, cook Bolognese and serve it with mountains of grated Parmigiano-Reggiano and a bottle of Brunello. If friends are over, make creamy potato and leek-laced pansotti together and bake a buttery and bubbly rhubarb-raspberry crisp. Serve everything on cheerful plates—it's time for some color. Definitely mix a martini. Read a short story, plant parsley, start running again (if you stopped, like me), find a hot bathing suit, and begin to make summer plans.

SPRING MENU

Preamble
Crispy Shrimp with Lemon Aioli

Sip
Super-Dirty Preserved-Lemon Martini

Salad
Butter Lettuce with Celery, Pistachio & Pecorino Toscano

Pastas
Good Pasta, Good Butter, End of Story

Potato Gnocchi with Baby Asparagus & Miso Butter

Wicked White Bolognese

Artichoke, Pea & French Feta Farfalle

Roasted Salmon & Fregola in a Zingy Dressing

Peppery Pappardelle with Pancetta & Mushrooms

Weeknight Wonder Rigatoni with Tuna, Fennel, Lemon & Olives

Creamy Potato, Caramelized Leeks & Gruyère Pansotti

Prosciutto & Ricotta Ravioli

For a Feast
Mighty Fine Skillet-Roasted Chicken

Dessert
Rhubarb & Raspberry Crisp with Vanilla Bean–Tangerine Ice Cream

Crispy Shrimp
with Lemon Aioli

Makes 4 to 6 servings

—

Lemon Aioli

2 egg yolks, at room temperature

1 garlic clove, finely grated

½ teaspoon Dijon mustard

1 tablespoon lemon juice,
or as needed

½ cup extra-virgin olive oil

½ cup neutral oil, such as
sunflower, grapeseed, or canola

¼ cup finely chopped flat-leaf
parsley

Kosher salt

Crispy Shrimp

1 pound (about 13) large
raw shrimp, with tails on

½ cup / 65g tipo 00 or
all-purpose flour

Kosher salt

¼ teaspoon freshly ground
black pepper

2 large eggs, lightly beaten

2 tablespoons water

1½ cups panko bread crumbs

2 teaspoons brown mustard seeds

2 teaspoons onion powder

Neutral oil, such as sunflower,
grapeseed, or canola, for frying

I dedicate these crispy, light morsels from the sea to my nan, who loved to start a night with a seafood appetizer and an ice-cold cocktail. Double-dipping in the lemon aioli is absolutely allowed, and don't skip a Super-Dirty Preserved-Lemon Martini (page 80). This combo will whet appetites and give the night an engine.

1   **To make the aioli:** In a small bowl, combine the egg yolks, garlic, Dijon mustard, and lemon juice. Place a dish towel under the bowl to keep it still as you vigorously whisk.

2   In a large measuring cup or in a plastic squeeze bottle, combine both oils. While continuously whisking the egg mixture, slowly add the oil, drop by drop. Once the mixture starts to thicken, add the remaining oil in a thin, steady stream. The consistency of the aioli will start to look like mayonnaise. When all the oil has been added, stir in the parsley and season with salt. If necessary, the aioli can be thinned by adding more lemon juice.

3   Store the aioli in an airtight container in the refrigerator for up to 3 days.

4   **To make the shrimp:** Place a wire rack on a baking sheet.

5   Peel the shrimp, leaving the tails attached. Using a small, sharp knife, butterfly the shrimp by cutting an incision down the back three-fourths of the way through the flesh, from head to tail. (Make sure not to cut *all* the way through.) Devein the shrimp by removing the digestive tract with the tip of the knife, then gently splay them open. Set aside.

6   On a plate, combine the flour, ½ teaspoon salt, and pepper.

7   In a small bowl, whisk the eggs and the water.

8   In another small bowl, combine the bread crumbs, mustard seeds, and onion powder and stir to incorporate.

9   Dip one shrimp into the flour mixture, then into the egg mixture, and finally into the bread crumb mixture, coating well. Place on a dinner plate or small baking sheet and repeat with the remaining shrimp.

10 Pour enough oil into a heavy-bottomed frying pan so it's about ½ inch deep and set over medium-high heat until it reaches 375°F. (If you don't have a thermometer, pop a few bread crumbs into the pan; if they sizzle, it's ready.)

11 Working in batches, carefully place several shrimp into the hot oil and fry until golden and crisp, approximately 1 minute on each side, then use a slotted spoon to transfer the shrimp to the prepared rack. Season with salt while still warm. Repeat with the remaining shrimp.

12 Serve the shrimp with aioli on the side.

Super-Dirty Preserved-Lemon Martini

Makes 1 drink

—

2 ounces gin

1 ounce dry vermouth

2 teaspoons green olive brine, plus 3 green olives

2 teaspoons preserved lemon brine or lemon juice, plus preserved lemon rind for garnishing

The addition of a few pink peppercorns sure would make this martini real pretty.

1   Place a martini glass in the freezer to chill for 5 minutes.

2   Pour the gin, vermouth, olive brine, and preserved lemon brine into a cocktail shaker or tall mixing glass filled with ice. Shake or stir until very well chilled, then strain into the prepared glass.

3   Garnish with a toothpick threaded with the olives and a sliver of preserved lemon rind and serve.

Butter Lettuce with Celery, Pistachio & Pecorino Toscano

Makes 4 servings

—

1 head butter lettuce

3 celery stalks, plus tender leaves

¼ cup extra-virgin olive oil

3 tablespoons lemon juice

1½ teaspoons honey

½ teaspoon Dijon mustard

¼ teaspoon kosher salt

¾ teaspoon freshly ground white or black pepper

⅓ cup salted pistachios, coarsely chopped

⅓ cup small mint leaves

⅓ cup shaved Pecorino Toscano, Pecorino Sardo, or Parmigiano-Reggiano

Flaky sea salt

This perennial salad ticks all the boxes: soft butter lettuce, crunchy celery, salty pistachios, lively mint, and sweet delicate Pecorino Toscano with a honey-Dijon dressing. The acidic dressing mingles so well with Good Pasta, Good Butter, End of Story (page 84). It's a great salad to serve when lots of friends come over. If anyone asks, "How can I help?" get them to assemble this pretty, pale green salad that requires no culinary chops.

1   Wash the lettuce and celery stalks and leaves in cold water to crisp them up, then dry everything thoroughly with a clean dish towel or in a salad spinner.

2   In a small bowl, whisk together the olive oil, lemon juice, honey, mustard, kosher salt, and half the pepper until well combined into a dressing.

3   Thinly slice the celery stalks on the diagonal, add to a small bowl with about half of the dressing, and let marinate for about 5 minutes.

4   In a larger bowl, toss the lettuce, marinated celery, pistachios, and mint with the remaining dressing.

5   Serve the salad topped with big shavings of the pecorino and celery leaves, and season with sea salt and the remaining pepper.

Good Pasta, Good Butter, End of Story

Makes 4 servings

Fresh pasta: 1 recipe Basic Egg Dough (page 16), cut into any shape (see pages 31 to 33)

Store-bought pasta: 14 ounces dried pasta, in pretty much any shape

—

6 to 8 tablespoons unsalted butter

Flaky sea salt

Freshly ground black pepper

Finely grated Parmigiano-Reggiano, Grana Padano, or Pecorino Romano for serving

—

TIP

Any pasta shape will work here, although this is how I use up maltagliati ("badly cut") pasta, those imperfect pieces of rolled dough abandoned at the edge of your board.

Is there anything better? Don't dismiss this disarmingly simple recipe: pasta and butter are the ultimate companions. Although homemade pasta needs very little to let it shine, a few knobs of good butter can take it to the sublime. Let me bang on about butter—big fan!—every now and again, I'll splurge on a local, boutique cultured butter or a European import with a higher percentage of butterfat. Finish the buttered pasta with cracked black pepper, a blanket of cheese, and flaky sea salt. Perhaps even a smattering of fresh, soft herbs? A generous squeeze of lemon juice and some zest for pasta al limone. But if it's for your lover, why not splurge and shave truffle on top?

1   Bring a large pot of lightly salted water to a boil. Add the pasta and cook until al dente, 2 to 3 minutes or according to package instructions if using store-bought.

2   In a large frying pan over medium-low heat, melt 6 tablespoons of the butter. Add ½ cup of the pasta water and simmer for a minute or two. Using a large spider or slotted spoon, transfer the pasta into the pan and toss until creamy and coated. Toss with the remaining 2 tablespoons butter or more pasta water to make it glossy, if needed. Remove from the heat, then season with salt and pepper.

3   Serve the pasta with Parmigiano or your choice of finely grated cheese on top.

Potato Gnocchi with Baby Asparagus & Miso Butter

Makes 4 servings

Fresh pasta: 1 recipe Potato Gnocchi (page 25)

Store-bought pasta: 1½ to 1¾ pounds potato gnocchi

—

1 bunch (about 9 ounces) tender asparagus, ends trimmed

3 tablespoons extra-virgin olive oil

6 tablespoons unsalted butter, at room temperature

1 shallot, finely chopped

½ teaspoon kosher salt

Freshly ground white or black pepper

3 garlic cloves, finely grated

1 to 2 tablespoons brown rice miso or other light miso

1 tablespoon finely chopped chives

Finely grated Parmigiano-Reggiano for garnishing

When asparagus spears are young, thin, and gorgeous, you just want to scratch their eyes out. Or you can pair them with this scrumptious garlic miso-butter sauce and pillowy potato gnocchi. Other spring veggies such as snap peas, sugar peas, or English peas all work well alongside or instead of asparagus. I like to serve this dish with a light Sicilian rosé made from the native grape Nerello Mascalese, which has a minerality that works with the umami of miso.

1   Cut off the pretty tips (the top 3 inches or so) of each asparagus spear and set aside. Finely slice the remaining asparagus on the diagonal.

2   In a large frying pan over medium-low heat, warm the olive oil and 2 tablespoons of the butter. Add the sliced asparagus stalks and the shallot and season with salt and pepper, sautéing until crisp-tender, about 3 minutes.

3   Add the garlic and the asparagus tips to the pan and sauté for 2 to 4 minutes more, then add the miso and remaining 4 tablespoons butter and stir to combine. Remove from the heat and keep warm.

4   Meanwhile, bring a large pot of lightly salted water to a boil. Add half of the gnocchi and cook for 2 to 3 minutes, or according to package instructions if using store-bought. When the gnocchi float to the surface, it's a good indication they're done. Pop one in your mouth to make sure it's cooked through. Using a slotted spoon, transfer the cooked gnocchi into the asparagus-miso mixture and gently stir to coat. Repeat with the remaining gnocchi, then add ¼ cup of the gnocchi water to the pan and toss gently to coat.

5   Serve the gnocchi with the miso-butter, garnished with the chives and grated Parmigiano.

Wicked White Bolognese

Makes 6 servings

Fresh pasta: 1 recipe Large-Batch Egg Dough (page 16), cut or shaped into fettuccine (see page 31) or garganelli (see page 32), or Simple Semolina Dough (page 27), shaped into orecchiette (see page 46) or cavatelli (see page 49)

Store-bought pasta: 1 pound dried macaroni, casarecce, or fettuccine

—

5 tablespoons extra-virgin olive oil, or as needed

3 tablespoons unsalted butter

4 ounces pancetta or prosciutto, finely diced

1 cup finely diced celery

1 cup finely diced carrot

1 cup finely diced yellow onion

4 garlic cloves, finely chopped

1 bay leaf

½ teaspoon kosher salt

Freshly ground black pepper

½ pound ground pork

½ pound ground veal or beef

½ cup good dry white wine

1 cup chicken stock

One 15-ounce can cannellini beans, rinsed and drained

1 cup heavy cream

1 cup finely chopped flat-leaf parsley, with tender stems and leaves

¼ cup finely chopped marjoram or thyme

1 to 2 tablespoons lemon juice

Finely grated Parmigiano-Reggiano for serving

All my friends love this! White Bolognese is a welcome change from the more ubiquitous red-sauce kind. If I'm honest, I think this version has more panache with its porky bits, veal, cannellini beans, and cream. This goes with just about any pasta shape, fresh or dried, but my absolute favorite is to have it with dried macaroni because every spoonful has equal portions of Bolognese and pasta, and I feel like a kid again.

1   In a large heavy-bottomed frying pan or Dutch oven over medium-low heat, combine the olive oil and butter and warm until the butter is melted. Add the pancetta, celery, carrot, onion, garlic, bay leaf; season with the salt and pepper; and sauté, stirring often, for 20 to 25 minutes. Make sure to really cook this soffritto down to get it caramelized. Transfer to a bowl and set aside.

2   Turn the heat to medium-high and add the pork, veal, and a splash more oil, if needed, to the pan. Cook the meat, breaking it up with a wooden spoon, until browned, 8 to 10 minutes.

3   Add the wine to the pan and deglaze, scraping up the browned bits with a wooden spoon. Let simmer for a few minutes, then add the chicken stock, beans, cream, parsley, marjoram, and pancetta-soffritto mixture. Lower the heat and let simmer for 10 to 15 minutes, stirring occasionally. Finally, stir in the lemon juice.

4   Meanwhile bring a large pot of lightly salted water to a boil. Add the pasta and cook until al dente, 2 to 3 minutes or according to package instructions if using store-bought. Using a large spider or slotted spoon, transfer the pasta into a large bowl and stir in a splash of olive oil to stop it from sticking together.

5   Serve the pasta topped with the Bolognese and grated Parmigiano.

Artichoke, Pea & French Feta Farfalle

Makes 4 servings

Fresh pasta: 1 recipe Basic Egg Dough (Spinach variation, see page 20), shaped into farfalle (see page 31)

Store-bought pasta: 14 ounces dried farfalle

—

2 cups oil-marinated artichokes, drained

½ cup extra-virgin olive oil

1 large white onion, halved and thinly sliced into half-moons

1 teaspoon kosher salt

2 garlic cloves, finely chopped

1½ cups sugar snap peas, trimmed and sliced diagonally in thirds

1 cup crumbled French feta

½ cup chopped dill

½ cup chopped mint

2 tablespoons lemon juice, plus zest of 1 lemon

Freshly ground black pepper

¼ cup pistachios, toasted and chopped

My friend Martine introduced me to French feta at Sahadi's deli in Brooklyn, and I've been hooked ever since. It's creamy and mellow and doesn't dominate a dish. I'm not going to make you prepare fresh artichokes because I'd prefer that you spend your time making spinach farfalle; just promise me you'll use oil-marinated artichokes. Crisp snap peas bring crunch, but snow peas or asparagus would work too. Tap into your inner food stylist and have fun plating the mélange of sugar snap peas, caramelized onions, pistachios, and lots of soft herbs. If using store-bought pasta, this comes together in a flash. I like to serve this with Grilled Anchovy-Marinated Lamb Chops (see facing page), but it can absolutely stand alone.

1   Slice each artichoke through the stem into bite-size pieces. Set aside.

2   In a large frying pan over medium-low heat, warm the olive oil. Add the onion and salt and sauté until soft and caramelized, about 10 minutes.

3   Meanwhile, bring a large pot of lightly salted water to a boil.

4   Add the garlic and snap peas to the onion, turn the heat to medium-high, and sauté until the peas are just crisp-tender, just a couple of minutes. Add the artichokes and warm through.

5   Add the farfalle to the boiling water and cook until al dente, 2 to 3 minutes or according to package instructions if using store-bought. Drain the pasta in a colander or use a large spider or slotted spoon to transfer the pasta to the artichoke mixture. Keep warm.

6   Add most of the feta, dill, and mint; the lemon juice; and some generous cranks of pepper to the pasta, and gently toss.

7   Serve the pasta topped with the pistachios, lemon zest, and remaining feta, dill, and mint.

Grilled Anchovy-Marinated Lamb Chops

Most of the time the artichoke-pea pasta is more than enough. But heartier appetites deserve a marinated lamb chop served on the side. Cut a frenched rack of lamb into eight individual chops. In a large bowl, stir together 5 mashed anchovies, 3 finely grated garlic cloves, 1 teaspoon kosher salt, the zest of 1 lemon, some freshly ground black pepper, and ⅓ cup extra-virgin olive oil. Add the lamb and let marinate for a few hours at room temperature, or cover and put in the fridge overnight and then bring to room temperature. Set a lightly oiled cast-iron skillet over high heat, or prepare a grill for high heat. Add the lamb and, depending on the thickness, cook for about 3 minutes, then flip and cook until browned but medium-rare, 3 to 4 minutes more. Cover and let rest until ready to serve with the pasta. (I'll tell you another day about the time I torched these on the grill when I got distracted by my phone. Moral of the story: Stay focused on your chops; they cook quickly.)

Roasted Salmon & Fregola in a Zingy Dressing

Makes 4 servings

Store-bought pasta: 14 ounces dried fregola Sarda, trofie, orzo, ditalini, or other small pasta

—

1-pound salmon fillet

2 tablespoons extra-virgin olive oil, plus ¼ cup

Kosher salt

Freshly ground black pepper

¾ cup crème fraîche

¾ cup plain Greek yogurt

1 tablespoon finely chopped preserved lemon, or the zest of 2 lemons

¼ cup lemon juice, plus lemon wedges for serving

3 tablespoons finely grated horseradish

2 tablespoons capers, plus 2 teaspoons caper brine

1 cup coarsely chopped dill

1½ cups watercress leaves, with tender stalks

Roasted salmon, tangy yogurt, and crème fraîche, lots of lemon, dill, watercress, and a little welcome kick from fresh horseradish make this pasta perfect for lunch or dinner. Fregola Sarda is a rustic Sardinian pasta made from durum wheat that's been rolled into very small balls, dried, and then toasted. It's similar to Israeli couscous, but it's more toothsome and nutty and is often served with seafood. It can be cooked like risotto, in a brothy soup, or in boiling water. If you can't get your hands on fregola, use another small, dried pasta, like orzo. Uncork an enchanting, far-too-easy-to-drink bottle of Vermentino and you've got yourself a meal.

1   Preheat the oven to 450°F. Line a baking sheet with parchment paper.

2   Pat the salmon dry with paper towels and place on the prepared baking sheet, skin-side down. Rub the fillet with the 2 tablespoons olive oil and season with 1½ teaspoons salt and some pepper. Roast until the internal temperature registers 145°F on an instant-read thermometer, 12 to 15 minutes.

3   Meanwhile, bring a large pot of lightly salted water to a boil. Add the pasta and cook until it's soft but still has a little chew (don't let it get mushy), 12 to 14 minutes, or according to package instructions. Drain the pasta in a colander and return it to the same pot. (If using fregola, rinse it under water and strain off any excess liquid to remove some of the starchiness.) Add the remaining ¼ cup olive oil and stir to coat.

4   In a small bowl, combine the crème fraîche, yogurt, preserved lemon, lemon juice, horseradish, capers, and caper brine to make a dressing. Season with salt and pepper.

5   Break the salmon into bite-size pieces, discarding any rogue bones, then add to the pasta. Stir in the dressing. Add some of the dill and watercress, reserving a little of each.

6   Serve the pasta garnished with the remaining herbs and lemon wedges on the side.

Peppery Pappardelle, Pancetta & Mushrooms

Makes 4 servings

Fresh pasta: 1 recipe Basic Egg Dough (page 16; or White Pepper variation, see page 20), cut into pappardelle or fettuccine (see page 31)

Store-bought pasta: 14 ounces dried pappardelle or fettuccine

—

2 tablespoons extra-virgin olive oil

6 ounces pancetta or thick bacon, diced

2 cups sliced button mushrooms

6 scallions, white and green parts, finely sliced

2 garlic cloves, grated

2 cups heavy cream

¼ teaspoon paprika (optional)

¼ teaspoon kosher salt

Freshly ground black pepper

4 tablespoons unsalted butter, at room temperature

¾ cup finely grated Parmigiano-Reggiano or Pecorino Romano, plus more for serving

I promise not one peppery pappardelle will be left behind on the plate. In fact, you might be tempted to lick the plate clean. I guarantee you'll crave this indulgence when your gas tank is low.

1   Bring a large pot of lightly salted water to a boil.

2   Meanwhile, in a large frying pan over medium heat, warm the olive oil. Add the pancetta and sauté for 4 minutes. Add the mushrooms, scallions, and garlic and continue to sauté until they have softened, 5 minutes more.

3   Add the cream, paprika (if using), salt, and some generous cranks of pepper to the pan. Lower the heat and maintain a gentle simmer. Make sure to scrape up any yummy, browned bits from the bottom of the pan to incorporate them into the cream sauce.

4   Add the pappardelle to the boiling water and cook until al dente, 3 to 4 minutes, or according to package instructions if using store-bought. Using a large spider or tongs, transfer the pasta into a large bowl, then add the butter and gently toss to melt. Finally, add the creamy pancetta sauce and Parmigiano, stirring to combine.

5   Serve the pasta with more cranks of pepper and a sprinkling of Parmigiano.

Weeknight Wonder
Rigatoni with Tuna, Fennel, Lemon & Olives

Makes 4 servings

Store-bought pasta: 14 ounces dried rigatoni, penne, farfalle, garganelli

—

1 lemon

¼ teaspoon kosher salt

1 tablespoon extra-virgin olive oil, plus 1 cup

1 small fennel bulb, shaved or thinly sliced

3 shallots, finely diced

5 garlic cloves, slivered

1 teaspoon fennel seeds, coarsely chopped

¼ to ½ teaspoon red pepper flakes

Freshly ground black pepper

One 7-ounce jar oil-marinated tuna, drained

⅓ cup pitted green olives, halved

4 cups loosely packed baby arugula

Shaved Parmigiano-Reggiano for serving

—

TIP

Substitute a couple tablespoons of the tuna oil for the extra-virgin olive oil if you want to double down on the tuna flavor.

I'm giving you a weeknight shortcut here by having you make this with dried pasta. And there's no need to confit tuna for hours—just use good oil-packed tuna (like Tonnino or Ortiz). Then the olive oil is infused with aromatics: shallots, lemon peel, garlic, fennel seeds, red pepper flakes, and black pepper—a time-saving combination, inspired by a recipe from *The Zuni Cafe Cookbook*. This heady mixture is tossed with barrel-chested rigatoni and topped with cool lemon-marinated fennel, arugula, and shaved Parmigiano-Reggiano to make it more of a pasta salad.

1   Peel the lemon, avoiding the white pith, and slice the peel into thin slivers. Juice the lemon and set aside.

2   In a small bowl, combine the lemon juice, salt, and 1 tablespoon olive oil and stir to incorporate. Add the shaved fennel and set aside to marinate.

3   In a large heavy-bottomed frying pan over medium-low heat, warm ¼ cup of the olive oil, then add the shallots and sauté for about 4 minutes. Turn the heat to very low; stir in the remaining ¾ cup olive oil, lemon peel slivers, garlic, fennel seeds, and red pepper flakes; season with black pepper; and gently infuse for 15 to 20 minutes, stirring occasionally. Add the tuna and olives and warm through, breaking apart the tuna with a fork.

4   While the olive oil is infusing, bring a large pot of lightly salted water to a boil. Add the pasta and cook until al dente, according to package instructions. Using a large spider or slotted spoon, transfer the pasta to the tuna mixture.

5   Add the arugula and about ½ cup of the pasta water to the mixture and stir gently to combine.

6   Serve the pasta with the marinated fennel and Parmigiano.

Creamy Potato, Caramelized Leeks & Gruyère Pansotti

Makes 6 servings

Fresh pasta: 1 recipe Large-Batch Egg Dough (page 16), prepared through Step 2

Review the techniques for filling pasta (see page 34) and shaping pasta (see page 37) before starting the recipe.

—

2 large russet potatoes, peeled and quartered

3 tablespoons unsalted butter

6 tablespoons extra-virgin olive oil

3 large leeks, white and light green parts, washed and finely chopped

8 scallions, white and green parts, thinly sliced on the diagonal

6 garlic cloves, finely diced, or 2 to 3 tablespoons finely diced green garlic

2 shallots, finely diced

1 teaspoon kosher salt

Freshly ground black pepper

1½ cups finely grated aged Gruyère

Zest of 1 lemon

1¼ cups crème fraîche

1¼ cups chicken stock

Finely grated Parmesan-Reggiano for serving

Flaky sea salt

—

TIP

While the dough is resting, make the filling.

Utterly delicious and comforting, this is the pasta equivalent of a pierogi. Imagine mashed potatoes, salty Gruyère, and tons of slowly cooked alliums all swaddled in delicate layers of egg dough, then tossed in a warm crème fraîche sauce. Spring alliums include garlic, leeks, scallions, onions, shallots, and chives—humble ingredients that, when cooked with care, take on another dimension. You'll end up with a bit of extra mashed potatoes; save them for a batch of Potato Gnocchi (page 25), or make it the cook's reward. Warning: Guard your potato pansotti because kids will definitely steal the last one from your plate. Bloody kids.

1   Bring a large pot of water to a boil. Add the potatoes and cook until tender, about 20 minutes or until you can poke a sharp knife into them and meet only a little resistance. Drain, return to the still-warm pot, and then dry them out by cooking over low heat for a few minutes. Turn off the heat, add the butter and, using a potato masher, mash until very smooth. No lumps, friends. Measure 2 cups of the mashed potatoes, and then put them aside in a medium bowl.

2   In a large frying pan over low heat, warm the olive oil. Add the leeks, scallions (reserving ¼ cup of the green tops), garlic, shallots, and kosher salt; season with pepper; and sauté until softened and lightly caramelized, about 10 minutes. Remove from the heat. Reserve ½ cup of the leek mixture in the pan, then transfer the rest to the bowl of mashed potatoes. Add the Gruyère and lemon zest and stir to combine well; this is your filling.

3   Roll out the pasta dough, then cut, fill, and shape into pansotti. Place the pasta, uncovered, on the prepared baking sheet, making sure they aren't touching.

4   Bring a large pot of lightly salted water to a boil.

5   Add the crème fraîche and chicken stock to the pan with the ½ cup leek mixture, turn the heat to low, and simmer, stirring occasionally, for about 5 minutes.

6   Working in batches, add the pasta to the boiling water and cook for 3 to 4 minutes. Remove one and check to see if it's done. Using a large spider or slotted spoon, transfer the pansotti into the warm, creamy leek sauce, turning gently to coat. Repeat with the remaining pansotti. (If your pan can't accommodate all the pansotti at once, serve it in rounds; just leave enough sauce for every last one.)

7   Serve the pasta with the reserved scallion tops, Parmigiano, and some pepper and sea salt scattered over the top.

Prosciutto & Ricotta Ravioli

Makes 6 servings

Fresh pasta: 1 recipe Large-Batch Egg Dough (page 16) or Peter Rabbit Pasta (see page 45, laminated with nasturtiums), prepared through Step 2

Review the techniques for filling pasta (see page 34) and shaping pasta (see page 37) before starting the recipe.

—

Filling

1¼ pounds whole-milk ricotta

3 ounces prosciutto, finely chopped

1 cup finely chopped tender nasturtium leaves, or ⅓ cup finely chopped chives

1½ teaspoons kosher salt

1½ teaspoons freshly ground black pepper

Zest of 1 lemon, plus 1 tablespoon lemon juice

Brown Butter

8 tablespoons unsalted butter, or as needed

1 tablespoon tender nasturtium stems or chives, finely chopped

1 handful nasturtium petals (optional)

—

TIP

While the dough is resting, make the filling.

This is a classic combination with a garden twist. I planted nasturtiums in my garden and, just as my mom had predicted, they took off and over. So, I started cooking with them—a lot! They found their way into these ravioli when I discovered that their spicy-sweet, horseradish-like flavor was superb with ricotta and prosciutto. (Chives would happily take their place if you don't have nasturtiums.) Sometimes I double down on the nasturtiums and laminate the tender petals and small leaves into the egg dough, tapping into eight-year-old Odette, who loved pressing flowers. Make sure to save a few petals to scatter on top for garnish.

1   **To make the filling:** In a medium bowl, combine the ricotta, prosciutto, nasturtium leaves, salt, pepper, lemon zest, and lemon juice and stir to incorporate.

2   Roll out the pasta dough, then cut, fill, and shape the ravioli. Place, uncovered, on the prepared baking sheet, making sure they aren't touching.

3   Bring a large pot of lightly salted water to a gentle boil.

4   **To make the brown butter:** In a large frying pan over medium-low heat, melt the butter until it starts to bubble and foam, smells nutty, and brown flecks appear. Stir in the nasturtium stems and keep warm.

5   Working in batches, add the ravioli to the boiling water and cook for 3 to 4 minutes. Remove one and check to see if it's done. Using a large spider or slotted spoon, transfer the ravioli into the brown butter, turning gently to coat. Repeat with the remaining ravioli, adding a little more butter to the pan if needed. (If your pan can't accommodate all the ravioli at once, just serve it in rounds. Just leave enough butter for every last ravioli.)

6   Serve the pasta with nasturtium petals on top, if desired.

Mighty Fine Skillet-Roasted Chicken

Makes 6 servings

—

3- to 3½-pound whole chicken (preferably organic)

Kosher salt

Freshly ground black pepper

Sprigs of sage, rosemary, thyme, or other woody herbs

1 lemon, quartered, plus zest of 1 lemon

4 tablespoons unsalted butter, at room temperature

1 fennel bulb or yellow onion, cut into wedges

1 garlic head, cut in half crosswise

3 tablespoons extra-virgin olive oil

I'm not reinventing the wheel with this recipe but rather giving you a crispy, succulent bird with a versatile flavor profile that works served alongside many of these pasta recipes. Alternatively, sometimes I spoon the leftover schmaltzy chicken jus over homemade fettuccine, add a knob of butter, and then top each serving with some shredded roast chicken, caramelized fennel, and garlic. That's living right there.

1   Preheat the oven to 400°F.

2   Bring the chicken to room temperature. Remove the giblets and then pat the chicken dry with paper towels. Season the cavity with salt and pepper. Place the herbs and half the lemon quarters inside the cavity, giving the lemons a squeeze.

3   Using your fingers, combine the lemon zest and butter. Gently lift the skin off the chicken and massage the lemon zest–butter mixture under the skin evenly. (Be careful not to tear the skin.) Pin the loose skin down with a toothpick at the neck to keep it in place. Tie the legs together with twine.

4   Place the chicken in a cast-iron skillet or small roasting pan. Nestle the fennel and garlic, cut-side down, around the chicken and splash them with the olive oil, rubbing it all over the chicken, and season everything generously with salt and pepper.

5   Place the skillet on the middle oven rack and roast for 55 to 65 minutes (15 to 20 minutes per 1 pound), making sure to turn the fennel and garlic once or twice. The chicken is done when the skin is golden and crisp and the juices run clear when cutting into the thickest part of the flesh, or registers 165°F on a meat thermometer.

6   Remove the chicken from the oven, drape with aluminum foil to keep warm, and let rest for 10 minutes.

7   Transfer the chicken to a cutting board, carve, and return it to the skillet, crispy-side up, along with any juices. Serve directly from the skillet with the remaining lemon quarters on the side for squeezing.

TIPS

For ultra-crispy skin, season the bird and then let air-dry by leaving it unwrapped in the fridge for a few hours or overnight. Bring to room temperature before cooking.

Sometimes I just put a few tablespoons of butter in the cavity and sprinkle the lemon zest over the skin, rather than under it.

Mash 4 anchovies into the butter for a bolder-flavored bird.

To make a jus, remove the chicken, fennel, and garlic from the skillet and set aside. Pour off most of the fat and reserve. Add 1½ cups dry white wine to the skillet, set over a medium-high heat, scrape up any of the yummy bits off the bottom with a wooden spoon, and let the liquid reduce by half, about 10 minutes. Season with a little salt and pepper, then strain the jus through a fine-mesh sieve. Drizzle the reserved chicken fat on freshly cooked pasta and toss to coat, then add as much jus as you'd like.

Rhubarb & Raspberry Crisp with Vanilla Bean–Tangerine Ice Cream

Makes 1 quart ice cream and one 9-inch crisp

Preparation: 20 to 30 minutes, plus chill and churn time (ice cream); 20 minutes (crisp)

—

Vanilla Bean-Tangerine Ice Cream

2 cups heavy cream

1 cup whole milk

Peel of ½ tangerine or small orange

½ vanilla bean, split and seeds scraped, pod reserved

6 egg yolks

¾ cup granulated sugar

½ teaspoon kosher salt

⅓ cup extra-virgin olive oil

½ teaspoon vanilla extract

Rhubarb & Raspberry Crisp

1 pound rhubarb, cut on the diagonal into 1-inch pieces

1 cup fresh or frozen raspberries

1 teaspoon orange zest, plus 2 tablespoons orange juice

2 tablespoons lemon juice

¼ cup granulated sugar

½ vanilla bean, split and seeds scraped, or 1 tablespoon vanilla extract

1 cup all-purpose flour

1 cup rolled oats

¾ cup lightly packed brown sugar

1½ teaspoons ground cinnamon

½ teaspoon kosher salt

8 tablespoons unsalted butter, diced

I'm always happy when rhubarb rolls out in spring. It's like running into a dear friend who never gets old and always looks glowing and radiant. Something about it just makes me want to bake. Its tart nature sings here with the sweet raspberries and buttery crisp—and let's be real, who doesn't love a crisp? Top it with a scoop of this luscious homemade ice-cream flavor that you won't find at the supermarket. If you've not had olive oil in ice cream before, you're in for a treat. (I won't judge you if you buy good vanilla bean gelato.)

1   **To make the ice cream:** In a large heavy saucepan over low heat, whisk together the cream, milk, citrus peel, and vanilla seeds and pod. Warm the mixture until simmering, then remove from the heat.

2   Meanwhile, in a large bowl, whisk together the egg yolks, granulated sugar, and salt until pale, 1 to 2 minutes. Slowly add the olive oil in a steady stream, whisking to incorporate.

3   Gradually pour the warm cream mixture into the eggs, whisking to combine. Return the mixture to the saucepan over low heat. Continuously stir this custard until it reaches 165°F on an instant-read thermometer, about 8 minutes. Whisk in the vanilla extract, then strain the custard through a fine-mesh sieve into a jug or bowl, discard the citrus peel and vanilla pod (make sure to squeeze any remaining vanilla seeds into the custard).

4   Transfer the mixture to the refrigerator to cool, about 4 hours.

5   When ready, pour the mixture into an ice-cream machine and churn according to the manufacturer's instructions. Place in a 1-quart container and transfer to the freezer.

6   **To make the crisp:** Preheat the oven to 350°F. Butter a 9-inch baking pan.

7   In a large bowl, toss the rhubarb and raspberries with the orange zest, orange juice, lemon juice, granulated sugar, and vanilla seeds, then spread out in the prepared pan.

8   In a medium bowl, combine the flour, oats, brown sugar, cinnamon, salt, and butter. Using your fingers, massage the mixture until the bits of butter are pea-size. Scatter this topping evenly over the fruit.

9   Bake the crisp until the topping is golden and the fruit is bubbly, about 45 minutes.

10 Serve the crisp warm, topped with a scoop of the ice cream.

TIPS

Chilling the ice-cream base before churning helps to stop ice crystals from forming. I've been known to skip this step if I plan on eating the ice cream immediately.

If there's a dessert that can handle seasonal improvisation, it's a crisp. All you need to know is this: For a 9-inch pan, use about 5 cups of fruit; experiment with it. In autumn or winter, I like apples, pears, and ginger; in the summer, it's stone fruit with blueberries or mango.

To make this gluten-free, use gluten-free oats and Bob's Red Mill 1-to-1 gluten-free baking flour, hazelnut flour, or almond flour instead of all-purpose flour.

Summer

If you do nothing else in summer except swirl tomatoes, basil, and burrata into homemade pasta, you'll be happy. Put your ice maker to work and sip a timeless spritz on a deck somewhere at sunset. Shuck some corn, and keep your eyes peeled for zucchini flowers to scatter on top of casarecce. Cook seafood because it's fast and light. You don't need to add much to branzino, shrimp, lobster, and clams. Just take some garlic, olive oil, lemon, herbs, maybe some crunchy bread crumbs, and then you're there. Make the real-deal passata with an old friend and talk—*really* talk. Take off your shoes, wear splendid hats, try building a champagne tower, lick salted-caramel ice cream, have a glass of chilled Nerello Mascalese in an outdoor shower, dance, and get some sun.

SUMMER MENU

Preamble

Nectarine & Cucumber Salsa with Burrata

Sip

Classic Summertime Spritz

Salad

Heirloom Tomato, Basil & Olive Croutons

Pastas

Beachy Alfresco Linguine alle Vongole

Spaghetti with Sun-Kissed Tomatoes, Ricotta & Crispy Prosciutto

Fried Zucchini & Basil Casarecce

Chopped Salad Pasta

Garlic Shrimp Mafaldine

Cacio e Pepe

Cavatelli with Sausage, Peppers & Oregano

Sweet Corn & Jalapeño Ravioli

Lobster Ravioli

Grilled Lemon, Garlic Butter & Herbed Orzo

For a Feast

Fabulous 15-Minute Branzino

Dessert

Salted Caramel Ice Cream with Chiacchiere

Nectarine & Cucumber Salsa with Burrata

Makes 4 servings

—

3 firm yellow nectarines, skin on, diced into ¼-inch cubes

2 small Persian cucumbers, diced into ¼-inch cubes

½ red onion, diced into ¼-inch cubes

½ red Thai chile, stemmed, seeded, and finely diced

2 tablespoons finely chopped mint, plus leaves for garnishing

¼ cup extra-virgin olive oil

¼ cup orange juice

2 tablespoons lemon juice

1 teaspoon whole-grain mustard

1 tablespoon maple syrup

½ teaspoon kosher salt

Freshly ground black pepper

8 ounces burrata

Flaky sea salt

This is the peaches-and-cream of salsa and so good for a cool starter on a blistering summer night. When the burrata ruptures and all the flavors mingle together, it's a moment to remember. Sometimes I'll use mangos instead of nectarines, but it's imperative that the fruit and cucumber be very firm and finely diced. That way you get the crunch and a mouthful of all the flavors in every bite. Pick up some fancy salty crackers, and you'll be good to go.

1   In a salad bowl, gently combine the nectarines, cucumbers, onion, chile, and mint.

2   In a small bowl, whisk together the olive oil, orange juice, lemon juice, mustard, and maple syrup. Season with the kosher salt and pepper. Pour half of this dressing onto the chopped salad and gently coat.

3   Place the burrata on top of the salad.

4   Just before serving, pour the remaining half of the dressing over the burrata, garnish with mint leaves, and sprinkle with a little sea salt.

Classic Summertime Spritz

Makes 1 drink

—

3 ounces Prosecco

2 ounces Cappelletti, Aperol, Campari, or other amaro

1 ounce club soda

1 slice tangelo, grapefruit, blood orange, or orange, plus peel for garnishing

—

TIP

To make a jugful, the recipe is as easy as 3, 2, 1: Three parts Prosecco, two parts amaro, and one part soda, with an accent of citrus on ice.

There are some really handsome-looking bottles of amaro on the market, some more bitter and herbaceous than others. I choose Cappelletti, but you could absolutely use Aperol or Campari instead. Feel free to tweak the following ratios to balance the intensity and bitterness. A squeeze or slice of citrus, like Minneola tangelo, calibrates this chilled Italian classic.

Fill your favorite glass with a handful of ice. Pour in the Prosecco, Cappelletti, and club soda, then add the citrus slice and stir. Garnish with the citrus peel and serve.

Heirloom Tomato, Basil & Olive Croutons

Makes 4 servings

—

4 cups cubed olive bread, ciabatta, or sourdough (½-inch cubes)

⅔ cup extra-virgin olive oil

1 cup basil leaves, plus more for garnishing

1½ pounds mixed heirloom tomatoes, cut into ¼- to ½-inch-thick slices

½ teaspoon kosher salt

Freshly ground black pepper

2 tablespoons sherry vinegar or champagne vinegar

Shaved Parmigiano-Reggiano for garnishing

Maldon smoked sea salt or flaky sea salt

I can't resist a mix of corpulent, knobbly, multicolored heirloom tomatoes. Cherokee Purple, Dwarf Emerald Giant, Ferris Wheel, Speckled Roman, Anna Russian, and Lucky Cross . . . so many varieties, such great names. If you can't get olive bread, just use any rustic loaf and add a handful of chopped olives instead. To plate, start with a smear of basil oil, then top with sliced tomatoes, crunchy crouton bits, and, finally, basil leaves that look as if they had blown in on the breeze. Nothing wrong with adding burrata or buffalo mozzarella to the mix either.

1   Preheat the oven to 350°F.

2   Place the bread cubes on a baking sheet and pour ⅓ cup of the olive oil over them, using your hands to help coat the bread. Bake for 5 minutes, then give them a shake, flip them over, and cook until golden and lightly crisp, 5 to 7 minutes more. Remove from the oven and, when they're cool enough to handle, chop these croutons in a mixture of different sizes: some chunky, some small and fine.

3   Finely chop the basil, transfer to a small bowl, and stir in the remaining ⅓ cup olive oil. Pour half the basil-oil mixture into a larger bowl, add about half the croutons to it, and toss to coat.

4   Spread the remaining basil oil across a large serving platter. Place the sliced tomatoes on top. Season with the kosher salt, pepper, and the vinegar so each tomato gets a few drops. Scatter the basil-soaked croutons over everything and then follow with the remaining croutons.

5   Serve the salad garnished with basil leaves, Parmesan, more pepper, and a sprinkling of sea salt.

Beachy Alfresco
Linguine alle Vongole

Makes 4 servings

Store-bought pasta: 1 pound dried linguine or spaghetti

—

¼ cup extra-virgin olive oil, or as needed

2 anchovies, drained and chopped

1 large shallot, finely diced

4 garlic cloves, finely chopped

3 ounces prosciutto, finely chopped

⅔ cup dry white wine

3 pounds littleneck clams, scrubbed and rinsed

1 cup finely chopped flat-leaf parsley

2 tablespoons unsalted butter

Zest of 1 lemon, plus 3 tablespoons lemon juice

2 teaspoons red wine vinegar or sherry vinegar

1 teaspoon kosher salt (depending on how salty your clam broth is)

Freshly ground black pepper

1 recipe Garlic Butter & Chile Bread Crumbs (see page 69)

After a long day of swimming and living your best life, you deserve to continue the dream by capping off the evening with a bowl of briny vongole. You can make homemade pasta, like linguine or fettuccine, but I fully back the ease and bite of store-bought pasta here. I've popped in some anchovies, prosciutto, a smidge of vinegar, and a smattering of garlic bread crumbs to give this classic clam pasta some oomph. As an Aussie girl who has spent many long days at the beach, I consider this the perfect après beach feast; absolutely polish off the rest of the wine with your meal.

1   Bring a large pot of lightly salted water to a boil.

2   In a large frying pan over medium heat, warm the olive oil. Add the anchovies and shallot and sauté for 3 to 4 minutes, then add the garlic and prosciutto and cook for another minute or two. Turn the heat to medium-high, add the wine and clams, then cover and cook for 5 to 8 minutes, occasionally jostling the pan to encourage the clams to open. Discard any clams that do not open.

3   Stir the parsley, butter, lemon zest, lemon juice, and vinegar into the clams and then season with the salt and pepper. Keep warm.

4   Meanwhile, add the linguine to the boiling water and cook for a minute or two shy of package instructions. Using a large spider or tongs, transfer the al dente pasta into the clam broth and toss well to coat. Depending on how much brine the clams have released, you may want to add a little pasta water or a splash of olive oil to loosen and marry everything.

5   Serve the pasta sprinkled with the bread crumbs on top.

Spaghetti with Sun-Kissed Tomatoes, Ricotta & Crispy Prosciutto

Makes 4 servings

Store-bought pasta: 14 ounces dried spaghetti, spaghettini, bucatini, or trenette

—

¼ cup extra-virgin olive oil, or as needed

3 garlic cloves

3 ounces prosciutto, thinly sliced

2 tablespoons unsalted butter

15 ounces Sungold or Early Girl tomatoes, halved or quartered

½ teaspoon kosher salt

1 cup loosely packed basil leaves

Freshly ground black pepper

¾ cup whole-milk or smoked ricotta

Shaved Parmigiano-Reggiano for serving

—

TIP

To make this dish vegetarian, top it with a few tablespoons of fried capers instead of the prosciutto.

This is a taste of summer sunshine and the epitome of simple. Sungold, Early Girl, or any small succulent tomato are splendid, served with a generous dollop of fresh ricotta and a sheet of fried prosciutto. Often, I'll swirl basil-infused oil around each plate if I have some on hand.

1   Line a plate with paper towels. In a large frying pan over low heat, warm the olive oil and garlic for about 4 minutes.

2   Turn the heat to medium, add 3 slices of the prosciutto to the pan, and gently panfry for 2 to 3 minutes, then flip and cook until crisp, about 1 minute more. Transfer the prosciutto to the prepared plate and repeat with the remaining 3 slices prosciutto, adding oil as needed. Remove and discard the garlic cloves.

3   Lower the heat, add the butter and tomatoes to the pan, and stir to combine. Keep warm.

4   Bring a large pot of lightly salted water to a boil. Add the pasta and cook until al dente, according to package instructions. Using a large spider or tongs, transfer the pasta into the warm tomatoes.

5   Add about ¼ cup of the pasta water to the pan and toss well to coat. Add the salt and ½ cup of the basil, then season generously with pepper.

6   Serve the pasta dolloped with the ricotta, some Parmigiano, and a crispy sheet of prosciutto on top. Finish with a splash of olive oil and the remaining ½ cup basil.

Fried Zucchini & Basil Casarecce

Makes 4 servings

Store-bought pasta: 1 pound dried casarecce or spaghetti

—

1½ pounds zucchini, thinly sliced into rounds

1¼ cups extra-virgin olive oil

1 shallot, finely diced

2 garlic cloves, minced

4 tablespoons unsalted butter, at room temperature

1 teaspoon lemon zest

⅔ cup basil leaves, coarsely chopped, plus leaves for garnishing

1½ cups finely grated Piave Vecchio or Parmigiano-Reggiano, plus more for serving

½ teaspoon kosher salt

Freshly ground black pepper

A few zucchini blossoms, sliced (optional)

Here's my riff on an Amalfi Coast classic: Spaghetti alla Nerano. I like to grow zucchini in my garden because they aren't fussy and will produce tender squash and beautiful flowers for me to cook with all summer long. Instead of spaghetti, I use casarecce, a sturdy, short, scroll-like pasta that captures sauce and can withstand the vigorous stirring that's needed to create the cheesy, creamy coating. I also use Paive Vecchio, a young, hard cheese that's not quite as salty as Parmigiano-Reggiano.

1   Pat the zucchini rounds with paper towels to remove excess moisture. Line a plate with paper towels.

2   In a frying pan over medium-high heat, warm 1 cup of the olive oil until it's nice and hot but not smoking. Working in batches, add the zucchini and fry until golden and crisp on both sides, 7 to 8 minutes per batch. Transfer the fried zucchini to the prepared plate. Keep warm.

3   Meanwhile, in another small frying pan over low heat, combine the remaining ¼ cup olive oil and shallot and sauté until softened, about 4 minutes, then add the garlic and cook for another minute or two. Remove from the heat.

4   Bring a large pot of lightly salted water to a boil. Add the casarecce and cook until al dente, according to package instructions. Reserve about 1½ cups of the pasta water, then drain the pasta in a colander and return it to the warm pot.

5   Off the heat, add the butter to the pasta, then stir in the shallot-garlic mixture, fried zucchini, lemon zest, and basil. Now gradually alternate between adding a little cheese followed by a little pasta water, while constantly stirring quite vigorously. (If you dump the cheese in all at once, you could end up with a clump.) Continue to add the cheese and as much pasta water as needed to create a creamy emulsion. Some of the zucchini will break up, but that's what we want. Add a little more pasta water, if needed, to make it glossy, or a splash of the zucchini-infused oil. Season with the salt and pepper.

6   Serve the pasta topped with a few basil leaves and zucchini blossoms, if desired.

Chopped Salad Pasta

Makes 4 servings

Store-bought pasta: 10 ounces dried ditalini or other small pasta, like macaroni or small conchiglie

—

2 tablespoons finely diced red onion

2 tablespoons red wine vinegar

2 tablespoons lemon juice

A splash of extra-virgin olive oil, plus ½ cup

Two 15-ounce cans chickpeas, drained and rinsed

4 ounces salami, cut into matchsticks

⅔ cup coarsely chopped pepperoncini

6 ounces fontina, cut into ¼-inch cubes

2 cups coarsely chopped radicchio or arugula

½ cup finely chopped flat-leaf parsley

1 tablespoon honey

1 teaspoon whole-grain mustard

8 sprigs thyme, stemmed

¾ teaspoon kosher salt

Freshly ground black pepper

This is perfect for a picnic, quick lunch, or easy dinner, and you don't have to turn on the oven! Every time you take a bite of this pasta salad, you'll get all the big, bold flavors of an antipasto platter—salami, chickpeas, fontina, pepperoncini—in one mouthful. Many of the ingredients are probably in your pantry already, but the recipe is very adaptable. If you don't have chickpeas, substitute butter beans; no salami, try oil-marinated tuna; or swap out the type of cheese. You get the gist.

1   In a small bowl, combine the onion, vinegar, and lemon juice and let marinate while you cook the pasta.

2   Bring a large pot of lightly salted water to a boil. Add the pasta and cook until al dente, according to package instructions. Drain the pasta in a colander, place in a large bowl, and add a splash of olive oil to stop it from sticking together.

3   Add the chickpeas, salami, pepperoncini, fontina, radicchio, and parsley to the pasta and toss to combine.

4   Whisk the ½ cup olive oil, honey, mustard, thyme, and salt into the onion-vinegar mixture and season with pepper. Pour over the pasta and toss to combine.

5   Serve the pasta on a platter and season with some cranks of pepper.

Garlic Shrimp Mafaldine

Makes 4 servings

Store-bought pasta: 1 pound dried campanelle, mafaldine, or angel hair pasta

—

1½ pounds large whole uncooked shrimp, with heads and tails on

6 tablespoons unsalted butter

3 tablespoons extra-virgin olive oil

2 large shallots, finely diced

¼ to ½ teaspoon red pepper flakes

8 garlic cloves, finely grated

⅔ cup dry white wine

Zest of 1 lemon, plus 2 teaspoons lemon juice

2 tablespoons finely chopped chives

1 cup finely chopped flat-leaf parsley

¾ teaspoon kosher salt

Freshly ground black pepper

1 recipe Garlic Butter & Chile Bread Crumbs (see page 69), for serving

—

TIP

Lobster-like rock shrimp would also be delicious. Use kitchen scissors to cut through the hard shells and then remove the veins.

Here, I've tried to re-create the sizzling garlic shrimp from Trieste, the Italian restaurant of my childhood. Look for shrimp with the heads on, since they add so much flavor to the sauce and give it a gorgeous coral-pink hue. If I can't get whole shrimp, I prefer to buy them unpeeled. Wavy ribbons of mafaldine or the curly nooks and crannies of trumpet-shaped campanelle allow the shrimp to nestle into every bite. A friend prefers it when I make this recipe with angel hair pasta, so use whatever pasta tickles your fancy. I'll often shower this with Garlic Butter & Chile Bread Crumbs. Either way, the heady aroma of butter, garlic, and shrimp cooking is one of life's greatest pleasures, so enjoy!

1 Bring a large pot of lightly salted water to a boil.

2 Cut off the head of each shrimp and set aside. Remove the tails, peel the shrimp, and discard the tails and shells. Using a sharp knife, make a shallow cut lengthwise along the back of each shrimp and then devein by removing the digestive tract with the tip of the knife, Cut each shrimp into three segments.

3 In a large skillet over medium-low heat, melt together the butter and olive oil, then add the shallots and red pepper flakes and sauté for a couple of minutes. Add the reserved shrimp heads and continue to sauté for 3 to 4 minutes more, occasionally pressing down slightly on the heads with a wooden spoon to release the juices. Remove and discard the heads and any rogue bits of shell.

4 Turn the heat to medium-high, add the shrimp and garlic, and sauté until the shrimp are just pink, just a couple of minutes. Add the wine, lemon zest, lemon juice, chives, and ½ cup of the parsley; season with the salt and pepper; and sauté until the wine has reduced by half, 4 to 5 minutes. Keep warm.

5 Add the pasta to the boiling water and cook until al dente, according to package instructions. Using a large spider or slotted spoon, transfer the pasta to the shrimp sauce along with about ½ cup of the pasta water and toss to coat. Serve the pasta sprinkled with the bread crumbs and garnished with the remaining ½ cup parsley.

Cacio e Pepe

Makes 2 servings

Fresh pasta: ½ recipe Simple Semolina Dough (page 27), shaped into pici (see page 50)

Store-bought pasta: 8 ounces dried spaghetti, bucatini, tonnarelli, or trofie

—

½ teaspoon black peppercorns

½ teaspoon white peppercorns

½ teaspoon pink peppercorns

3 tablespoons unsalted butter, at room temperature

1 tablespoon extra-virgin olive oil

½ teaspoon kosher salt

1 cup finely grated Pecorino Romano, plus more for serving

What's not to love about cacio e pepe (cheese and pepper)? It's a bestseller! However, successfully pulling off cacio e pepe can be a little challenging if not executed well. Read the tips in order to avoid ending up with a big clump of split cheese. I cheat and add a little oil and butter (because when does adding either hurt?) that makes emulsifying the sauce easier. I often use different types of pecorino: Romano, Sardo, and Toscano, or I'll mix pecorino with Parmigiano-Reggiano. Then I really break the rules with the pepper by adding a little more personality in that department. Instead of using just black pepper, I play with a trio of peppers: fruity, sweet pink peppercorns; bright, herbaceous white peppercorns; and pungent black peppercorns. If you don't have all three types of pepper, black will be just fine.

1   Bring a large pot of lightly salted water to a boil. Add the pasta and cook until al dente or a minute or two shy of package instructions if using store-bought.

2   While the pasta cooks, place all the peppercorns in a mortar and pestle and smash into very small fragments (not too much dust, not too many chunks).

3   When the pasta is al dente, reserve at least 1½ cups of the pasta water, drain the pasta in a colander, and then return it to the still-warm pot.

4   Off the heat, add the butter, olive oil, salt, and all but a pinch of the pepper to the pasta and stir to combine. Add a splash of the pasta water, then hold your hand up high over the pot and gradually sprinkle a couple tablespoons of the pecorino over the pasta while stirring quite vigorously with a large wooden spoon (you may need to steady the pan). Repeat this sequence a few times, until you have incorporated all the pecorino and about 1 cup of the water (or just as much as needed to create a creamy, emulsified sauce).

5   Serve the pasta with that last pinch of pepper and more grated pecorino.

TIPS

Cacio e pepe is easier to execute with a smaller quantity of pasta; that is why this recipe serves just two (generously).

Sturdy, store-bought durum wheat semolina pasta can withstand constant tossing and stirring.

Don't forget to reserve some pasta water! It's crucial!

Cacio e pepe is about creating an emulsion; combining fat with water to create a creamy sauce. This requires continuously stirring or tossing.

Don't rely on pre-grated cheese here; grate your own, very finely, using a Microplane or the finest side of a box grater. Working *off the heat*, gradually add the cheese, while tossing and incorporating the pasta water, so the cheese doesn't get too hot and split. If you dump it in all at once, you could end up with a clump.

If you want to try tossing the pasta rather than stirring, use a frying pan with deep sides; it'll give the pasta plenty of room to cook and then help contain it as it's tossed, so it doesn't end up on the floor.

Cavatelli with Sausage, Peppers & Oregano

Makes 4 servings

Fresh pasta: 1 recipe Simple Semolina Dough (page 27), shaped into cavatelli (see page 46), or Potato Gnocchi (page 25)

Store-bought pasta: 14 ounces short dried pasta such as cavatelli, fusilli, or casarecce

—

¼ cup extra-virgin olive oil

3 links (12 to 14 ounces) sweet or hot Italian sausage, casings removed

1 yellow onion, finely diced

1 bay leaf

¾ teaspoon kosher salt

Freshly ground black pepper

4 garlic cloves, thinly diced

3 tablespoons tomato paste

½ cup chicken stock

3 bell peppers (mix of red, orange, and yellow), seeded and finely diced

1 tablespoon finely chopped fresh oregano

2 tablespoons sherry vinegar

½ cup heavy cream

Finely grated Parmigiano-Reggiano for sprinkling

Red pepper flakes for sprinkling

My son, Ned, loves this! It's like having all the flavors of an outstanding salsiccia (Italian sausage) pizza but in pasta. Sweet or hot sausage and slow-cooked peppers and onions are bound together with a splash of stock and cream. Make sure to dice the bell peppers finely and be patient as they slowly caramelize. I like to use cavatelli here, since it cradles the sauce. Before diving in, add a sprinkle of red pepper flakes and keep the Parmigiano at the ready.

1   In a large heavy-bottomed frying pan or Dutch oven over medium heat, warm the olive oil. Add the sausage, onion, and bay leaf; season with the salt and pepper; and cook for 10 minutes, breaking the meat into small pieces with a wooden spoon.

2   Add the garlic to the pan and sauté for 1 minute, then add the tomato paste and continue to cook for another minute or two.

3   Pour the chicken stock into the pan and deglaze, scraping up the browned bits with a wooden spoon. Add the bell peppers and oregano, turn the heat to medium-low, and continue to cook, stirring often, until the bell peppers are caramelized, 20 to 25 minutes. Add the vinegar and then stir in the cream to combine. Discard the bay leaf. Keep warm.

4   Bring a large pot of lightly salted water to a boil. Add the pasta and cook until al dente, 3 to 4 minutes or according to package instructions if using store-bought. Using a large spider or slotted spoon, transfer the pasta into the sausage-pepper sauce. Pour in about 1 cup of the pasta water and stir to loosen the sauce, making it creamy and coating the pasta.

5   Serve the pasta with a sprinkling of Parmigiano and red pepper flakes.

Sweet Corn & Jalapeño Ravioli

Makes 6 servings

Fresh pasta: 1 recipe Large-Batch Egg Dough (page 16), prepared through Step 2

Review the techniques for filling pasta (see page 34) and shaping pasta (see page 37) before starting the recipe.

—

Filling

4 ears sweet corn, or 3 cups frozen corn kernels

3 tablespoons unsalted butter

2 tablespoons extra-virgin olive oil

1 large shallot, finely chopped

2 jalapeños, stemmed, seeded, and finely chopped

1½ cups finely grated Parmigiano-Reggiano

⅔ cup whole-milk ricotta

½ cup basil leaves

1½ teaspoons kosher salt

Freshly ground black pepper

Corn Butter

8 tablespoons unsalted butter, or as needed

⅓ cup corn (reserved from filling)

1 jalapeño, stemmed, seeded, and sliced into thin rounds

Basil leaves for topping

—

TIP

While the dough is resting, make the filling.

When my family moved from New York and drove across the country to San Francisco, I plotted where we'd eat. One of the most memorable meals was at Rolf and Daughters in Nashville. Even though we'd never been there before, we felt like regulars. The entire meal was phenomenal, especially the homemade pasta; in particular, a sweet corn–jalapeño agnolotti. The moment that I got to California, I tried to re-create that summertime belle from the South. Instead of making agnolotti, which can require more advanced pasta-shaping skill, I make a simple ravioli. These work well as a main or as a side, served with Skirt Steak with Olive Gremolata (see page 226). Turn on Johnny Cash and imagine your hand is hanging out the car window, dancing in the warm breeze, while you roll and fill these cover girls.

1   **To make the filling:** Bring a large pot of salted water to a boil. Add the corn and cook until tender, 6 to 8 minutes for fresh corn or 4 minutes for frozen. Drain and, when cool enough to handle, cut the kernels off the cobs. Reserve ⅓ cup kernels for the corn butter.

2   In a small frying pan over low heat, melt together the butter and olive oil. Add the shallot and chopped jalapeños and sauté until softened, about 5 minutes.

3   In a food processor, combine the shallot-jalapeño mixture, corn, Parmigiano, ricotta, and basil; season with the salt and pepper; and puree until smooth. Transfer to a large bowl.

4   Roll out the pasta dough, then cut, fill, and shape into mezzelune ravioli or other stuffed pasta of your choice. Place, uncovered, on the prepared baking sheet, making sure they aren't touching.

5   Bring another large pot of lightly salted water to a gentle boil.

6   **To make the corn butter:** Meanwhile, in a large frying pan over medium-low heat, melt the butter until it starts to bubble and foam. Add the ⅓ cup corn and sauté until golden, about 3 minutes. Remove from the heat and stir in the jalapeño rounds. Keep warm.

7   Working in batches, add the filled pasta to the boiling water and cook for 3 to 4 minutes. Remove one and check to see if it's done. Using a large spider or slotted spoon, transfer the ravioli to the corn butter, turning gently to coat. Cook the remaining ravioli and transfer to the pan, adding a bit more butter if needed. (If your pan can't accommodate all the ravioli at once, serve it in rounds; just leave enough butter mixture for every last one.)

8   Serve the ravioli topped with a few small basil leaves.

Lobster Ravioli

Makes 4 servings

Fresh pasta: 1 recipe Large-Batch Egg Dough (page 16; or Saffron variation, see page 20), prepared through Step 2

Review the techniques for filling pasta (see page 34) and shaping pasta (see page 37) before starting the recipe.

—

Filling

8 tablespoons unsalted butter

2 tablespoons extra-virgin olive oil

1 celery stalk, finely diced

1 shallot, finely diced

1 large garlic clove, finely diced

½ cup dry white wine

13 ounces cooked lobster, shredded

1 tablespoon finely chopped chives

1 tablespoon finely chopped dill

1 tablespoon finely chopped flat-leaf parsley

1 cup whole-milk ricotta

Zest of 1 lemon, plus 4 teaspoons lemon juice

1 teaspoon kosher salt

Freshly ground black pepper

Chive Brown Butter

8 tablespoons unsalted butter, or as needed

1 tablespoon finely chopped chives

Extra-virgin olive oil for drizzling

—

TIPS

Substitute crab for lobster meat, if that's more your kind of crustacean.

While the dough is resting, make the filling.

This recipe is a lesson in delayed gratification. The test is to *not* eat all the lobster meat before you've filled the pasta. These parcels are worth the splurge when you need to indulge. The filling uses a splash of wine, so why not pick up a special bottle of white to sip on while you roll, fill, and eat these treats? I'm saying this makes four servings so you won't have to share it among six people.

1   **To make the filling:** In a frying pan over low heat, melt together the butter and olive oil. Add the celery, shallot, and garlic and sauté until softened, about 8 minutes. Add the wine and deglaze the pan, scraping up the browned bits with a wooden spoon, then simmer until it has reduced by half. Stir in the lobster, chives, dill, and parsley, breaking up any large chunks. Remove from the heat and let cool slightly.

2   In a large bowl, combine the lobster mixture, ricotta, lemon zest, and lemon juice; season with the salt and pepper; and stir to incorporate.

3   Roll out the pasta dough, then cut, fill, and shape into round ravioli or pansotti or other stuffed pasta of your choice. Place, uncovered, on the prepared baking sheet, making sure they aren't touching.

4   Bring a large pot of lightly salted water to a boil.

5   **To make the brown butter:** In a large frying pan over medium-low heat, melt the butter until it starts to bubble and foam, smells nutty, and brown flecks appear. Stir in the chives and keep warm.

6   Working in batches, add the ravioli to the boiling water and cook for 3 to 4 minutes. Remove one and check to see if the filling is lovely and warm. (You're welcome.) Using a large spider or slotted spoon, transfer the ravioli into the brown butter, turning gently to coat. Repeat with the remaining ravioli, adding a bit more butter to the pan if needed. (If your pan can't accommodate all the ravioli at once, serve it in rounds; just leave enough butter for every last one.)

7   Serve the ravioli finished with a drizzle of olive oil.

Grilled Lemon, Garlic Butter & Herbed Orzo

Makes 4 servings

Store-bought pasta: 1 pound dried orzo

—

3 tablespoons extra-virgin olive oil

6 tablespoons unsalted butter

4 garlic cloves, quartered

2 lemons, halved

⅔ cup finely chopped flat-leaf parsley

¼ cup finely chopped basil leaves

3 tablespoons finely chopped chives

1½ teaspoons kosher salt

Freshly ground black pepper

—

TIP

If making both this orzo and Fabulous 15-Minute Branzino, infuse the butter and garlic for both recipes together in the same saucepan.

What is it about orzo? It's addictive; you just can't stop eating it, even when you're full. The combo of seared or grilled lemons and garlic-infused butter tossed with orzo is so satisfying that it just might take you back to childhood, and it's especially well-paired with Fabulous 15-Minute Branzino (facing page).

1   Bring a large pot of lightly salted water to a boil. Add the orzo and cook until al dente, according to package instructions, then drain in a colander, return to the still-warm pot, and add 1 tablespoon of the olive oil to stop it from sticking.

2   While the orzo is cooking, in a small saucepan over low heat, melt the butter. Add the garlic and warm gently for about 5 minutes.

3   In a small cast-iron skillet over medium-high heat, warm the remaining 2 tablespoons olive oil. Add the lemon halves, cut-side down, and sear until the flesh has charred, about 5 minutes. Remove the lemons, squeeze their juice through a fine-mesh strainer into the pasta, and stir to combine.

4   Remove the garlic from the butter and discard. Stir the parsley, basil, chives, salt, and generous cranks of pepper into the infused garlic butter.

5   Pour the garlic butter over the orzo, stir well, and serve.

Fabulous 15-Minute Branzino

Makes 4 servings

—

2 whole branzino (about 1 pound each), scaled, cleaned, and cavities gutted

4 tablespoons unsalted butter

6 garlic cloves

Kosher salt

1 lemon, cut into ½-inch slices and then into half-moons

1 cup flat-leaf parsley leaves

2 to 3 tablespoons extra-virgin olive oil

Freshly ground black pepper

—

TIPS

If you can't buy branzino, try bream, snapper, or an extra-large sand whiting.

Tying the branzino in kitchen twine helps contain the filling. It's not essential here but more decorative. Simply cut a long piece of twine and wrap and tie a knot around the tail, continue to wrap it a few times around the body, then tie another knot near the gills to secure the twine.

Let's pretend that we're at a Mediterranean seaside restaurant, having a languid meal of freshly caught fish, drinking bucket-loads of chilled Roero Arneis with zippy lemon vibes and slightly salty character. Whole branzino is a mild, delicate white fish that cooks in no time, either in the oven or on the grill. I serve this with Grilled Lemon, Garlic Butter & Herbed Orzo (facing page) or other summer pastas.

1   Preheat the oven to 500°F.

2   Using paper towels, pat dry the skin and cavity of the branzino.

3   In a small saucepan over low heat, melt the butter. Add the garlic and give everything a little time together to become one. After infusing, set aside.

4   Line a large baking sheet with parchment paper. Working directly on the baking sheet, season the cavities of each fish with ½ teaspoon salt. Add 2 tablespoons of the melted butter, 3 garlic cloves, 3 lemon slices, and ½ cup of the parsley into each cavity.

5   Rub the skin of each fish with about 1 tablespoon of the olive oil and season generously with salt and pepper.

6   Roast the fish until the skin is crisp, or the internal temperature registers 145°F on an instant-read thermometer, about 15 minutes. Remove from the oven and let rest for a few minutes.

7   Serve the branzino topped with the remaining lemon slices.

To Grill Branzino

Preheat the grill to 400°F (medium-high) and then lightly oil it. Put the garlic and butter in a heat-proof bowl and place on the grill as it's warming up, so that the garlic is infused into the butter as it melts. Remove from the grill or move to the top shelf. When the grill is hot, place the prepared fish diagonally on the grates to get those fabulous grill marks. Close the lid; cook undisturbed (so the skin doesn't stick) for 7 minutes, then carefully flip and continue cooking until the internal temperature registers 145°F on an instant-read thermometer, about 7 minutes more. (Be careful not to overcook. A clue that the fish is done: its eyes will become cloudy.) Make sure to char a few halved lemons, cut-side down, to serve on the side.

Salted Caramel Ice Cream
with Chiacchiere

Makes 1 quart ice cream and about 100 chiacchiere

Preparation: 20 to 30 minutes, plus chill and churn time (ice cream); 20 minutes (chiacchiere)

—

Salted Caramel Ice Cream

¾ cup granulated sugar

¼ cup water, or as needed

2 cups heavy cream

1 cup whole milk

6 egg yolks

¼ cup dark muscovado sugar (or granulated sugar)

1 teaspoon vanilla extract

½ teaspoon kosher salt

The best investment that I've made for preparing desserts at home is an ice-cream machine. It allows for this part of the meal to be simple, yet special, with very little effort. You can create all sorts of unique flavors or classics, like salted caramel. Muscovado sugar makes a caramel that's rich in flavor and color. (If you don't have muscovado sugar, you can just use granulated sugar.) Caramel on the brink waits for no one, so mise en place is essential. I usually make the ice-cream base ahead of time and then churn it while we eat, so everyone gets to enjoy the divine mouthfeel of freshly churned ice cream. The chiacchiere—delicate, fried, sugar-dusted Italian pastries that are so easy and fun—edge this dessert into completely charming. I used to beg my mom for them when we'd go to the Italian deli. To make them, roll and cut the dough the way you would egg dough, then fry and dust with confectioners' sugar. Leftovers are great with your morning coffee. I like to cap off a night with a glass of Moscato d'Asti, a sparkling Italian dessert wine, so use it in this recipe where a sweet wine is called for. To be honest, you can't really identify it; it's just my excuse to indulge in a bottle of this effervescent ending.

1   **To make the ice cream:** In a heavy-bottomed light-colored saucepan (so you can monitor the color of the caramel) over medium heat, combine the granulated sugar and water. Don't stir but swirl the pan occasionally so it cooks evenly. If sugar crystals form around the pan, use a pastry brush dipped in water to dissolve them. Cook until the sugar turns a dark amber, 11 to 13 minutes. (Watch it in the final minutes, there's a fine line between perfect and burnt caramel.) Take the pan off the heat immediately and carefully pour in the cream and milk and whisk to combine.

2   In a medium bowl, whisk together the egg yolks and muscovado sugar, making sure to remove any lumps. Temper the yolks by pouring in some of the hot caramel-cream mixture, while whisking constantly. Then return the mixture to the saucepan.

3 Turn the heat to medium-low and cook this custard, stirring continuously, until it has thickened slightly, or registers 165°F on an instant-read thermometer, 4 to 5 minutes. Stir in the vanilla and kosher salt. Strain the custard through a fine-mesh sieve into a bowl.

4 Transfer the mixture to the refrigerator to cool, about 4 hours.

5 When ready, pour the mixture into an ice-cream machine and churn according to the manufacturer's instructions. Place in a 1-quart container and transfer to the freezer.

Continued

Salted Caramel Ice Cream with Chiacchiere, continued

Chiacchiere

2¼ cups tipo 00 flour or
all-purpose flour

2 tablespoons granulated sugar

1 teaspoon baking powder

½ teaspoon kosher salt

4 tablespoons unsalted butter,
melted

⅓ cup Moscato d'Asti or
other sweet wine

2 teaspoons orange zest

1½ teaspoons vanilla extract

1 large egg, beaten

Neutral oil, such as sunflower,
grapeseed, or canola, for
deep frying

Confectioners' sugar for dusting

Smoked or regular Maldon sea salt

—

TIPS

You will need a pasta rolling machine to make chiacchiere.

If you just want to enjoy the concept of this dessert without expending the energy, buy good, salted caramel ice cream and/or chiacchiere. That's fine with me.

6   **To make the chiacchiere:** In a large bowl or the bowl of a stand mixer, combine the flour, granulated sugar, baking powder, and kosher salt and mix on low speed. Add the butter, wine, orange zest, vanilla, and egg and continue mixing until a dough comes together in a ball.

7   Place the dough on a clean, dry, lightly floured work surface and knead until the dough comes together in a smooth ball, just a couple minutes. Cover well in plastic wrap and let chill in the fridge for 30 minutes.

8   Lightly flour a baking sheet. Divide the chilled dough into four equal parts. (Wrap any dough you're not working with in plastic so it doesn't dry out). Take one portion of dough, flatten it between your palms, and then feed it through a pasta machine's widest setting on low speed. It will be a bit crumbly, that's okay; it will come together the more you roll it. Fold the dough in half and repeat this at the same setting until the dough is no longer crumbly and becomes smooth. Roll the sheet down through the settings to #6 or #7.

9   On a lightly floured surface, cut the sheet of dough into 4 by 2-inch rectangles, preferably with a decorative scalloped ravioli cutter. Cut a 2-inch slit down the middle of each rectangle. Place on the prepared baking sheet. Repeat with the remaining dough.

10   Fill a deep heavy-bottomed pot with a couple of inches of oil and set over high heat until it registers 375°F on an instant-read thermometer. Working in batches, carefully place the dough strips into the oil and fry until light golden and crisp, 10 to 20 seconds. Using a slotted spoon, transfer the chiacchiere to a wire rack. Repeat with the remaining strips. Let cool, then dust generously with confectioners' sugar. Transfer to an airtight container and store at room temperature for a day or two.

11   When ready to serve, scoop the ice cream into bowls, sprinkle with a bit of sea salt, and place a chiacchiere with each one. Pass the remaining chiacchiere on the side because everyone will want more.

Autumn

Fire up the oven. It's time for baked pastas. Your Saturday is well spent making trays of lasagna and listening to classical music or catching up on podcasts. Make sure that one night you serve mac and cheese with schnitzel. That's a combo you'll want to revisit. Add an arugula salad and it becomes a complete meal. Work the pantry staples, anchovies, lentils, tinned tomatoes, porcini mushrooms. Kids might not like bottarga, but they'll love garganelli with vodka sauce, or meatballs and spaghetti. Keep your eyes peeled for a large vintage platter that makes seafood spaghetti marinara look like a million bucks. Don't forget to make garlic bread! Set panna cotta in a bunch of motley small glasses or in one large pie dish. Either way, it's always pretty and feels good in your mouth. While the panna cotta is setting, sweep leaves, take a bath, laugh your head off, take your time, wear wool, and just be you.

AUTUMN MENU

Preamble
Marinated Peppers,
Gruyère & Hazelnut Dip

Sip
Sanpellegrino 75

Salad
All about Arugula Salad

Pastas
Garganelli with Vodka Sauce

Beet & Carrot Agnolotti with Sage-Hazelnut Butter

Umbrian Lentil & Porcini Ragù

Midnight Fettuccine with Seared Scallops

Seafood Marinara (Frutti di Mare)

Meatballs with Mama's Red Sauce & Spaghetti

Luxe Mac & Cheese

Tagliatelle with Lamb, Fennel & Olives

"Yum, You're Lovely!" Classic Bolognese Lasagna

For a Feast
Superior Schnitzel

Dessert
Sesame & Honey Panna Cotta

Marinated Peppers, Gruyère & Hazelnut Dip

Makes approximately 2 cups

—

½ cup unsalted whole hazelnuts

1 cup oil-marinated red peppers, drained and coarsely chopped

3 ounces aged Gruyère, grated

2 garlic cloves

2 teaspoons red wine vinegar

½ cup extra-virgin olive oil

1 teaspoon kosher salt

Freshly ground black pepper

This combination of oil-marinated red peppers, toasted hazelnuts, and aged Gruyère, whizzed together into a dip, is addictive. Once you start dipping, you'll be hovering. Serve it with charcuterie and crudités (see following), crackers, or grilled bread, or keep it lowbrow and bust open a bag of crinkle-cut potato chips with a crisp Italian Pilsner.

1   In a small skillet over medium-low heat, toast the hazelnuts until fragrant. Let cool slightly, then place in a clean dish towel and rub the nuts vigorously to remove the skins.

2   In a food processor, combine the hazelnuts, red peppers, Gruyère, garlic, and vinegar and pulse to blend. Gradually pour the olive oil through the tube and continue pulsing until combined. Season with the salt and generous cranks of black pepper. Place in one of your favorite bowls to serve.

Charcuterie

I love cured meats sliced wafer-thin, be it soppressata, salami, prosciutto, mortadella, or coppa. For an appetizer platter, estimate about 3 ounces of mixed charcuterie per person. When pairing with cheese, assemble a balanced combination of flavors and textures. Try a dry, salty cheese, like aged Gouda, with a mellow mortadella or San Daniele prosciutto or soft buffalo mozzarella or mild fontina, paired with a spicy soppressata or salami.

Crudités

In spring or summer, I like to serve dip with a selection of raw seasonal vegetables: young rainbow carrots; petite radishes with their tops still on; trimmed sugar snap peas; Belgian endive leaves; crisp Persian cucumber spears; peeled kohlrabi, cut into matchsticks; and lightly blanched green beans or asparagus. To get raw or blanched vegetables ultra-crisp, briefly shock them in ice water and then pat dry before arranging and serving.

Sanpellegrino 75

Makes 1 drink

—

Citrus, smoked, or regular flaky salt
1 lemon wedge
4 ounces Prosecco
2 ounces gin
4 ounces citrus-flavored
Sanpellegrino (such as Limonata)
Citrus twist for garnishing

I'm mixing two of my favorites, a French 75 with citrus Sanpellegrino. Aranciata, Pompelmo, Clementine, and Peach would also work, but it's hard to go past Limonata. Have all the liquids chilled before mixing, and crush the ice to get a granita-like vibe going. I discovered citrus salt was a great addition to the rim of this cocktail after picking up an orange salt at the Ballaro market in Palmero, Sicily. You could also muddle in a little mint or basil.

1   Place a collins or highball glass in the freezer to chill for 5 minutes. Put a few teaspoons of salt on a small plate.

2   Run the lemon wedge around the rim of the glass and then dip the glass in the salt.

3   Put a large handful of ice in a clean dishcloth and give it a number of good whacks with a mallet, rolling pin, or a sturdy metal spoon until crushed. Place the ice in the prepared glass.

4   Pour the Prosecco, gin, and Sanpellegrino into a glass and stir.

5   Garnish with the citrus twist and serve.

All about Arugula Salad

Makes 4 servings

—

5 cups arugula

3 tablespoons extra-virgin olive oil

2 tablespoons balsamic vinegar

Freshly ground black pepper

Shaved Parmigiano-Reggiano
for topping

Flaky sea salt

I debated including this arugula salad in the book because it is *just so simple.* However, this is the salad that I throw together the most when making homemade pasta because it requires nothing of me. Do splurge on good extra-virgin olive oil, vinegar, and Parmigiano-Reggiano. Occasionally, I use different varieties of arugula: astro arugula, broad-leafed Italian cress, delicate baby arugula, wild arugula, or peppery rocket arugula. If you come across arugula microgreens, you're in for a treat; those little guys pack a punch and will make you feel like a chef when plating them. This salad goes well with roasted squash or shaved fennel. If I'm in the mood for fruit, I'll add slices of persimmon, pear, stone fruit, or segments of blood orange. But I'm very picky when it comes to putting fruit in my salad. It has to be perfectly ripe for it to make the cut.

1   In cool water, wash the arugula, dry thoroughly in a clean dish towel or salad spinner, and then put in a large serving bowl.

2   In a small bowl, whisk together the olive oil and vinegar, then season with some generous cranks of pepper.

3   Just before serving, toss the arugula with the oil and vinegar. Top with Parmigiano and a sprinkle of sea salt to finish.

Garganelli with Vodka Sauce

Makes 4 servings

Fresh pasta: 1 recipe Large-Batch Egg Dough (page 16), shaped into garganelli (see page 32)

Store-bought pasta: 1 pound dried garganelli or penne

—

3 tablespoons extra-virgin olive oil

1 shallot, finely diced

2 garlic cloves, grated

1 small red Thai chile, stemmed, seeded, and finely diced, or ½ teaspoon red pepper flakes

3 tablespoons tomato paste

¼ cup vodka

¾ cup heavy cream

½ cup grated Parmigiano-Reggiano, plus more for topping

⅓ cup coarsely chopped basil leaves, plus small leaves for topping

1 teaspoon kosher salt

—

TIP

Omit the fresh chile and serve red pepper flakes on the side if you have little ones who are sensitive to spice.

My daughter Opal once made a recipe for pasta vodka sauce that she found on the internet, put in too much vodka, and then didn't cook it off. It was so strong that it ripped our heads off and made her brother Ned a hater. She has since learned about cooking off alcohol and has mastered my version of this crowd pleaser. Ned has come around, and we never have leftovers. Garganelli is a great shape for kids to make. If you don't make your own pasta, use dried pasta on a weeknight, and this recipe will come together in a flash.

1   Bring a large pot of lightly salted water to a boil.

2   In a large heavy-bottomed frying pan over medium heat warm the olive oil. Add the shallot, garlic, and chile and sauté just until translucent, about 3 minutes.

3   Add the tomato paste to the pan and cook for another couple of minutes, then pour in the vodka and cook it off for a couple minutes more.

4   Add the cream to the pan and bring to a gentle simmer for a couple of minutes. Lower the heat and keep the sauce warm.

5   Add the pasta to the boiling water and cook until al dente, 2 to 3 minutes or according to package instructions if using store-bought. Using a large spider or slotted spoon, transfer the pasta into the warm sauce, along with ¼ cup of the pasta water, and toss to coat. Stir in the Parmigiano and basil, then season with the salt.

6   Serve the pasta topped with additional Parmigiano and small basil leaves.

Beet & Carrot Agnolotti with Sage-Hazelnut Butter

Makes 6 servings

Fresh pasta: 1 recipe Large-Batch Egg Dough (page 16), prepared through Step 2

Review the techniques for filling pasta (see page 34) and shaping pasta (see page 37) before starting the recipe.

—

3 medium carrots, peeled and diced into small cubes

2 small red beets, peeled and diced into small cubes

8 tablespoons unsalted butter

3 tablespoons extra-virgin olive oil, plus more for drizzling

2 shallots, finely diced

2 garlic cloves, finely diced

2 teaspoons kosher salt

1¼ teaspoons ground red Kampot pepper or black pepper, or as needed

2 tablespoons crème fraîche

⅔ cup hazelnuts, coarsely chopped

⅓ cup sage leaves

Finely grated Parmigiano-Reggiano for garnishing

Flaky sea salt

—

TIPS

Steam the beets and carrots so the filling doesn't get too wet.

Cambodian Kampot pepper comes in black, white, and red peppercorns. Here, I use the red variety that's left on the vine to fully ripen; its fruity sweetness opens to a fleeting heat.

The color, oh, the color . . . just you wait until you bite into these and discover the glamorous hue that awaits. There's something about these agnolotti that makes me feel that I could be the kind of woman who has red lipstick and a mirror always at the ready. Caramelized shallots, garlic, and crème fraîche are swirled into an earthy beet-carrot puree for the filling, then the petite parcels are topped with a buttery mélange of crisp sage and hazelnuts, making these to die for. Oh . . . and if taking on agnolotti feels like too much, just make these into pansotti or mezzelune.

1   Put an inch or two of water in a large pot, insert a steamer basket, and cover with a lid. Set over medium-high heat and bring to a boil. Add the carrots and beets, re-cover, and steam until the vegetables are very soft, about 25 minutes.

2   Meanwhile, in a large heavy-bottomed frying pan over medium-low heat, melt together 4 tablespoons of the butter and the olive oil. Add the shallots and cook until softened, 4 to 5 minutes. Then add the garlic, kosher salt, and pepper and cook for a few minutes more. Remove from the heat.

3   In a food processor, combine the beets, carrots, crème fraîche, and half of the butter-shallot mixture and puree until smooth, occasionally scraping down the sides with a rubber spatula. Transfer this filling to a bowl to cool.

4   Roll out the pasta dough, then cut, fill, and shape into agnolotti. Place, uncovered, on the prepared baking sheet, making sure they aren't touching.

5   Bring a large pot of lightly salted water to a gentle boil.

6   Return the frying pan with the remaining shallot mixture to medium-high heat and add the remaining 4 tablespoons butter, the hazelnuts, and sage. Sauté until the sage is lightly crisped, 1 to 2 minutes.

7   Working in batches, add the pasta to the boiling water, cook for
     3 to 4 minutes, and then drain.

8   Serve the pasta drizzled with a little olive oil. Spoon the hazelnut-
     shallot mixture over the top and garnish with additional pepper,
     some Parmigiano, and sea salt.

Umbrian Lentil & Porcini Ragù

Makes 4 servings

Fresh pasta: 1 recipe Basic Egg Dough (page 16), shaped into strozzapreti (see page 32) or fettuccine (see page 31)

Store-bought pasta: 14 ounces dried strozzapreti, or fusilli

—

1 ounce dried porcini mushrooms

3 cups boiling water

2 tablespoons extra-virgin olive oil, or as needed

1 small onion, finely diced

1 small fennel bulb, finely diced

2 carrots, finely diced

1 celery stalk, finely diced

2 garlic cloves, finely chopped

1 bay leaf

½ teaspoon fresh thyme

Kosher salt

Freshly ground black pepper

2 tablespoons unsalted butter

½ cup Umbrian or Puy lentils, rinsed in cold water

One 14-ounce can San Marzano crushed tomatoes

¼ cup chicken stock or vegetable stock or boiling water

1 tablespoon red wine vinegar

½ cup finely chopped flat-leaf parsley

½ cup crème fraîche or sour cream

If you haven't cooked with Umbrian lentils before, they might just become your favorite; they cook quickly yet retain their shape and bite. Cooked with a handful of vegetables, tomatoes, and earthy dried porcini mushrooms, this hearty, wholesome ragù is a cool-weather keeper. It can be served alone or with pasta.

1   In a medium bowl, combine the mushrooms and boiling water and let soak for 15 minutes. Place a fine-mesh sieve over a bowl and strain the mushrooms, reserving the liquid. Squeeze any excess liquid from the mushrooms, then coarsely chop; set aside the liquid and mushrooms.

2   In a large Dutch oven over medium-low heat, warm the olive oil. Add the onion, fennel, carrots, celery, garlic, bay leaf, and thyme; season with the salt and pepper; and sauté until softened, about 10 minutes.

3   Add the mushrooms and butter to the pot. Once the butter has melted, add the lentils, tomatoes, reserved mushroom liquid, and chicken stock, then cover and simmer, stirring occasionally, for 30 to 40 minutes.

4   When the lentils are tender yet still have some bite, turn off the heat and stir in the vinegar and parsley. Adjust the seasoning if needed, then cover to keep warm.

5   Bring a large pot of lightly salted water to a boil. Add the pasta and cook until al dente, about 4 minutes or according to package instructions if using store-bought. Drain the pasta in a colander, return it to the still-warm pot, and toss with a little olive oil to keep it from sticking.

6   Serve the pasta with a generous ladle of ragù and dolloped with the crème fraîche.

Midnight Fettuccine with Seared Scallops

Makes 4 servings as a main, or 6 servings as a side

Fresh pasta: 1 recipe Basic Egg Dough (Squid Ink variation, see page 20), cut into fettuccine (see page 31)

Store-bought pasta: 14 ounces dried or fresh squid ink fettuccine

—

10 tablespoons unsalted butter

¼ cup extra-virgin olive oil, plus 2 tablespoons

½ cup finely grated bottarga, plus more for serving

1 shallot, finely diced

3 garlic cloves, finely diced

½ teaspoon ground white pepper

Kosher salt

⅓ cup dry white wine

½ cup finely chopped flat-leaf parsley

Zest of 1 lemon, plus lemon juice for serving

1 pound sea scallops

Freshly ground black pepper

—

TIPS

You can buy cuttlefish or squid ink at your fishmonger or Italian specialty grocers; both inks will work. I usually use 2 to 3 tablespoons of ink when making both egg dough recipes. If you want it darker, add a few more tablespoons.

Bottarga can also be purchased at an Italian grocer or online. If you can't get it, melt a few anchovies into the butter sauce instead.

A little bit Joan Jett, a little bit Parisian Hôtel Costes, a lotta va-va-voom . . . the color from cuttlefish or squid ink gives the pasta a dramatic, smoky, dark hue. Funnily enough, the ink doesn't add any detectable flavor in pasta—leave that to the scallops and bottarga (cured mullet roe). Nestled in the glossy black fettuccine, the seared, juicy, sweet scallops and sea-salty bottarga add umami and opulence. It's great as a starter, served in small nests with a scallop or two at center stage, or for dinner on an amorous evening in. Pop a bottle of blush-colored bubbles and you've got yourself a night to remember.

1   Bring a large pot of lightly salted water to a boil.

2   In a large frying pan over medium-low heat, combine 8 tablespoons of the butter and the ¼ cup olive oil. When the butter has melted, add the bottarga, shallot, garlic, white pepper, and 1½ teaspoons salt and sauté until the shallot has softened, about 4 minutes. Add the wine, parsley, and lemon zest and cook for a few minutes more to reduce the wine by half. Remove from the heat and keep warm.

3   Pat the scallops dry with a paper towel, then season lightly with salt and black pepper. Set a large skillet (preferably cast-iron) over high heat. When the pan is really hot, add the remaining 2 tablespoons butter and 2 tablespoons olive oil. When the butter has melted, add the scallops to the pan without crowding them (if necessary, cook in two batches). Sear without disturbing, until the bottoms are golden brown, about 2½ minutes. Flip the scallops and continue cooking on the other side until caramelized, another couple of minutes. Remove from the pan and keep warm.

4   Add the pasta to the boiling water and cook until al dente, 2 to 3 minutes or according to package instructions if using store-bought. Using a large spider or tongs, transfer the pasta into the butter-bottarga sauce. Toss well to coat, adding a splash of pasta water to loosen if needed.

5   Using tongs, swirl the pasta into nests on plates, then top with the scallops and a squeeze of lemon juice. Finally, and best of all, generously grate bottarga over each serving.

Seafood Marinara
(Frutti di Mare)

Makes 6 servings

Fresh pasta: 1 recipe Large-Batch Egg Dough (page 16), cut into fettuccine (see page 31)

Store-bought pasta: 1 pound dried fettuccine, spaghetti, or linguine

In my early twenties, I waitressed at Dolomiti's, a family-run Italian restaurant. It was like being in an Elena Ferrante novel. Friday nights were outrageously busy and sweaty. The restaurant, like many Italian restaurants in Australia, was started by the first wave of Italian emigrants. The father was a man of few words, who tended lovingly to all the gelato that he made. The corpulent mother was gregarious and warm. She would pitter-patter around the restaurant, wiping tables, greeting guests, working the cash register, and thanking the regulars for coming. When I worked there, their two daughters were in charge. Before and during service, the sisters ferociously battled each other somewhere between the front of house and the kitchen. They worked hard and cooked with consistency and pride. At the end of the night, wine was poured, cigarettes lit, and the tensions would dissolve into laughter. I'd walk home, completely done in, often carrying spaghetti marinara and gelato. To this day, I believe Dolomiti's made the best seafood spaghetti marinara. It had a little heat from the chiles and just the right amount of seafood tossed in. It tasted fabulous, even when eaten out of a plastic takeaway container after midnight. I'm not sure how Lina, the matriarch, would judge my rendition, but I think it's pretty close. I make fresh fettuccine for special occasions and use store-bought spaghetti when I'm channeling Lina. It's never a bad idea to have garlic bread (see page 70) at the table for this one.

Continued

Seafood Marinara (Frutti di Mare), continued

½ cup extra-virgin olive oil, plus more for serving

6 anchovy fillets, chopped

1 shallot, finely chopped

3 garlic cloves, finely chopped

2 tablespoons finely chopped fresh oregano

1 teaspoon red pepper flakes

One 28-ounce can San Marzano crushed tomatoes

Kosher salt

Freshly ground black pepper

1½ pounds mussels, shells scrubbed, debearded

1 pound medium-large shrimp, peeled and deveined

½ pound squid, cleaned and cut into ¼-inch rings

½ cup finely chopped flat-leaf parsley

⅓ cup finely chopped basil leaves

2 teaspoons lemon zest, plus 1 tablespoon lemon juice

1 Bring a large pot of lightly salted water to a boil.

2 Meanwhile, in a very large frying pan over low heat, gently warm the olive oil. Add the anchovies and cook slowly, mashing them with a wooden spoon until they are melted into the oil. Turn the heat to medium and add the shallot, garlic, oregano, and red pepper flakes and sauté until the shallot has softened, about 4 minutes. Add the tomatoes, season with salt and pepper, and let simmer for 8 to 10 minutes.

3 Add the mussels, shrimp, and squid to the tomato sauce, then cover and turn the heat to medium-high. Cook until the shrimp turn pink, occasionally jostling the pan to encourage the mussels to open, 4 to 6 minutes. (I love the sound the mussels make when the shells knock together—it's as if they're tap dancing.) Turn off the heat and discard any mussels that haven't opened.

4 Transfer the mussels in their shells to a large bowl and, when cool enough to handle, pluck the mussels out of their shells and return them to the sauce. Set aside a few still in their shells to use as a garnish. Discard the empty shells.

5 Add the parsley, basil, lemon zest, and lemon juice to the sauce and stir to incorporate. Taste and adjust the seasoning if needed.

6 Add the pasta to the boiling water and cook until al dente, 2 to 3 minutes or according to package directions if using store-bought. Drain in a colander before transferring to the seafood marinara. Toss until the pasta is well coated and the seafood is distributed.

7 Serve the pasta garnished with the reserved mussels and a splash of olive oil.

Meatballs with Mama's Red Sauce & Spaghetti

Makes 6 servings

Store-bought pasta: 1 pound dried spaghetti

—

Meatballs

1½ cups day-old bread, like ciabatta, cut into 1-inch cubes

1⅓ cups whole milk

¼ cup extra-virgin olive oil, plus more drizzling

1 small yellow onion, finely diced

5 garlic cloves, finely diced

4 teaspoons fennel seeds, crushed

3 tablespoons finely chopped oregano leaves

1 carrot, finely diced

2 pounds ground pork

¾ cup finely grated Parmigiano-Reggiano

1 extra-large egg, beaten

¾ cup finely chopped flat-leaf parsley

2 teaspoons kosher salt

2 teaspoons ground white pepper

Freshly ground black pepper

1 recipe Mama Sordo's Red Sauce (page 58), Luxurious Pomodoro in a Flash (page 59), or 24 to 28 ounces of your favorite store-bought red sauce

Finely grated Parmigiano-Reggiano for topping

Oregano leaves for topping (optional)

This is a well-engineered, classic meatball. Some things belong together—pork and fennel being an exemplary combination. I crush the fennel seeds and sauté them with the onion, garlic, and carrot mixture to evenly distribute their fabulousness throughout the meatballs. You can absolutely panfry meatballs if eating them crispy and crunchy is your preferred way, but I tend to cook them in the oven, since it's quick, hands-off, and less mess. I'm not going to ask you to make spaghetti from scratch, because honestly, store-bought is better here.

1   **To make the meatballs:** Preheat the oven to 450°F. Lightly oil a large baking sheet.

2   In a bowl, soak the bread in the milk.

3   In a frying pan over low heat, warm the olive oil. Add the onion, garlic, fennel seeds, and oregano and sauté for a couple of minutes, then add the carrot and continue to cook until softened, about 8 minutes more.

4   In a large bowl, combine the pork, Parmigiano, egg, parsley, and onion-carrot mixture; season with the salt, white pepper, and black pepper; and stir to incorporate.

5   Squeeze out and discard the excess milk from the bread and add the soaked bread to the mixture. Use your hands to break up the bread and mix everything together until well combined.

6   Using your hands, roll approximately twenty-four meatballs (slightly larger than golf balls) and place them on the prepared baking sheet. Drizzle a little olive oil over the tops, then roast in the oven for 12 to 14 minutes. Remember, cooking these in the oven means the bottoms of the meatballs brown first, so check to see if they're golden, then carefully roll them over and continue browning for 3 to 4 minutes more.

7   Meanwhile, in a large Dutch oven or large pot over low heat, warm the red sauce. Transfer the meatballs into the sauce and continue to cook over low heat for 10 to 15 minutes.

TIPS

A couple tablespoons of chopped pine nuts or raisins can be added to the meat mixture to give the meatballs more personality.

Substitute beef for the pork or use a 1:1 combination.

Oiling your hands will make rolling the meatballs easier.

8   Bring a large pot of lightly salted water to a boil.

9   Add the spaghetti to the boiling water and cook until al dente according to package instructions. Drain the pasta in a colander, then return it to the still-warm pot, drizzling a little olive oil on it to keep the pasta from sticking together.

10 Serve the spaghetti topped with the saucy meatballs, lots of Parmigiano, and a few oregano leaves, if desired.

Luxe Mac & Cheese

**Makes 6 servings as a main,
or 8 servings as a side**

Store-bought pasta: 1 pound mezzi
rigatoni or garganelli

—

6 tablespoons extra-virgin olive oil,
or as needed

4 tablespoons unsalted butter

4 tablespoons truffle butter

½ cup all-purpose flour

5 cups whole milk, warmed

1¼ cups finely grated
Parmigiano-Reggiano

1 cup finely grated Gruyère

4 teaspoons Dijon mustard

1 teaspoon kosher salt

½ teaspoon ground white pepper

Freshly ground black pepper

8 ounces pancetta or bacon, diced

2 large shallots, finely diced

6 scallions, white and green parts,
finely sliced

1 garlic clove, finely diced

1 bay leaf

1 cup heavy cream

½ cup finely chopped flat-leaf
parsley

¾ cup fresh bread crumbs
(see page 69)

—

TIPS

If you can't find truffle butter, use
8 tablespoons unsalted butter and
a truffle Dijon mustard (like Maille).

If truffles aren't your thing, just use
8 tablespoons unsalted butter.

Make this recipe vegetarian by
substituting mushrooms for the
pancetta.

Bordering on hedonistic, a good mac and cheese should be saucy, like an Alfredo, and require a spoon to scoop up the creamy luxury. No need to make fresh pasta; dried is best here. Mezzi rigatoni, a short, dried, tubular pasta, is ideal; it holds the decadent sauce without greedily absorbing it, as macaroni can do. Around the holidays, if friends are over, I'll serve this dish as a starter with a bottle of searing, bubbly champagne—a surprising combination that works as the acidity and bubbles cut through the rich, cheesy goodness.

1   Preheat the oven to 350°F.

2   Bring a large pot of salted water to a boil. Add the pasta and cook until al dente, about 3 minutes shy of package instructions, then drain in a colander. Return the pasta to the still-warm pot and add a splash of the olive oil to keep the pasta from sticking together.

3   In a large heavy-bottomed saucepan over low heat, melt together the unsalted butter and truffle butter. Add the flour and cook for 2 minutes, whisking constantly. Gradually whisk in the milk until smooth. When this béchamel is velvety and has a consistency of heavy cream, add the Parmigiano, Gruyère, mustard, salt, white pepper, and generous cranks of black pepper and stir to combine.

4   In a frying pan over medium-low heat, combine 3 tablespoons olive oil and the pancetta and sauté for a minute or two, then add the shallots, scallions, garlic, and bay leaf and continue cooking until softened, about 8 minutes. Discard the bay leaf and set the pan aside.

5   Add the pancetta mixture to the pasta, then stir in the béchamel, heavy cream, and parsley. Pour into either two 8-inch square baking dishes, one 9 by 13-inch baking dish, or multiple small ramekins.

6   In the frying pan that the pancetta was cooked in, warm the remaining olive oil. Add the bread crumbs and cook for 1 minute to coat them and then sprinkle them on top of the mac and cheese.

7   Bake for approximately 20 minutes or until bubbling around the edges . . . and this mac and cheese is ready to be devoured.

Tagliatelle with Lamb, Fennel & Olives

Makes 6 servings

Fresh pasta: 1 recipe Large-Batch Egg Dough (Whole-Wheat variation, see page 20), cut into tagliatelle (see page 31)

Store-bought pasta: 1 pound whole-wheat or regular tagliatelle, fettuccine, or garganelli

—

1 pound deboned lamb shoulder, cut into 1-inch cubes

Kosher salt

Freshly ground black pepper

3 tablespoons extra-virgin olive oil, or as needed

1 large fennel bulb, diced; fronds reserved for garnishing

1 yellow onion, diced

1 large carrot, diced

3 garlic cloves, finely chopped

2 tablespoons tomato paste

½ cup dry white wine

1 cup beef stock

One 28-ounce can San Marzano crushed tomatoes

1 large sprig rosemary

3 tablespoons pitted Picholine or other green olives, halved

Greek feta for topping

When I was growing up in Australia, Sunday dinners always included a roast leg of lamb. This recipe is an ode to those super-hearty, boldly flavored meals that punctuated the weekends. Patiently building your ragù is how flavors develop, so take your time cooking the onion and fennel low and slow; similarly, cook the tomato paste until it darkens a bit. If you've never had pitted Picholine olives, you'll want to try them. They are one of my favorites: green, salty, and petite. They'll vanish in a flash as you snack on them while cooking. I like to serve this ragù with whole-wheat pasta, a sprinkling of feta cheese, and a bottle of Sangiovese.

1   Generously season the lamb all over with salt and pepper.

2   In a large heavy-bottomed Dutch oven over medium-high heat, warm the olive oil. When the oil shimmers, add the lamb and sear for 5 to 7 minutes on each side (work in batches if needed, so you don't crowd the pan). Remove the lamb from the pan and set aside.

3   Turn the heat to medium; add the fennel, onion, carrot, ½ teaspoon salt, and a bit of pepper; and sauté, stirring occasionally, until softened, 5 to 7 minutes. Add the garlic and cook for 1 minute more.

4   Add the tomato paste to the pan and stir well, cooking for 2 to 3 minutes, letting the mixture caramelize and darken a bit. Add the wine and deglaze the pan, scraping up the browned bits with a wooden spoon. Let simmer and reduce by half.

5   Add the beef stock, tomatoes, and rosemary to the pan, then return the lamb and any accumulated juices. Cover, turn the heat to low, and cook until the lamb is melt-in-your-mouth tender and falling apart, 2 to 2½ hours. Discard the rosemary. Using two forks, pull the meat apart. Stir in the olives and season this ragù with a little more salt, if needed.

6 Meanwhile, just before serving, bring a large pot of lightly salted water to a boil. Add the pasta and cook until al dente, 2 to 3 minutes or according to package instructions if using store-bought. Drain the pasta in a colander, then return it to the still-warm pot, drizzling in a little olive oil to keep the pasta from sticking together.

7 Serve the pasta topped with the ragù, a crumble of feta, and garnished with a few fennel fronds.

"Yum, You're Lovely!" Classic Bolognese Lasagna

Makes 8 servings

Fresh pasta: 1 recipe Large-Batch Egg Dough (page 16; or the Spinach variation, see page 20), cut into lasagna sheets (see page 31) that fit a 9 by 13-inch baking dish

Store-bought pasta: 12 ounces dried lasagna sheets

—

Classic Bolognese

½ cup extra-virgin olive oil

1 onion, finely diced

1 carrot, finely diced

1 fennel bulb, finely diced

2 garlic cloves, finely diced

2 anchovies

3 tablespoons tomato paste

One 28-ounce can San Marzano crushed tomatoes

1 pound ground pork

1 pound ground beef

1¼ cups chicken stock, or as needed

3 tablespoons balsamic vinegar

½ cup finely chopped basil leaves

½ cup finely chopped flat-leaf parsley

1 teaspoon kosher salt

Freshly ground black pepper

I know, I know . . . the dishes, the counter space, the layering, the time . . . I get it. Baked pastas are a labor of love. But you can't beat a lasagna made with homemade pasta. They also are an impressive, hands-off way to feed a crowd if prepared in advance. So, let's *do* this. The best Bolognese lasagnas that I've eaten had a hint of vinegar hidden in the silky layers (so I always add a little to mine) and plenty of white sauce, which is why I use both fresh ricotta and a béchamel. A robust peppery bottle of Australian Shiraz or Chianti would round out this meal perfectly. Unbuckle your belts!

1   **To make the Bolognese:** In a large frying pan over medium heat, warm ¼ cup of the olive oil. Add the onion, carrot, fennel, garlic, and anchovies and sauté gently until softened, about 10 minutes. Add the tomato paste and cook for a couple of minutes, then add the tomatoes and cook for 5 minutes more. Remove from the heat, let cool slightly, and then pour the mixture into a large food processor or blender and pulse until smooth.

2   In the same frying pan over medium-high heat, warm the remaining ¼ cup olive oil. Add the pork and beef and sauté, breaking up the meat with a wooden spoon, until browned, about 10 minutes. Add the chicken stock, vinegar, tomato mixture, basil, and parsley; season with the salt and pepper; and stir to combine. Cover, turn the heat to low, and let simmer, stirring occasionally, for about 30 minutes. Add a little more stock or water if the Bolognese becomes dry. Remove from the heat.

Continued

"Yum, You're Lovely!" Classic Bolognese Lasagna, continued

Lasagna Béchamel

6 tablespoons unsalted butter

⅓ cup all-purpose flour

3¾ cups whole milk, warmed

1 cup finely grated Parmigiano-Reggiano

1 teaspoon kosher salt

⅛ teaspoon ground nutmeg

Freshly ground black pepper

Extra-virgin olive oil for drizzling

1½ cups finely grated Parmigiano-Reggiano

Freshly ground black pepper

12 ounces whole-milk ricotta, strained

Basil leaves for finishing

3 tablespoons unsalted butter

3   **To make the béchamel:** In a large heavy-bottomed saucepan over low heat, melt the butter. Add the flour and cook for 2 minutes, whisking constantly. Gradually whisk in the milk until smooth. When the béchamel is velvety and has the consistency of heavy cream, add the Parmigiano, salt, nutmeg, and some cranks of pepper and whisk to combine. Set aside.

4   Preheat the oven to 400°F.

5   Bring a large pot of lightly salted water to a boil. Working in batches, blanch four sheets of fresh pasta at a time until just softened, for 1 to 2 minutes. (If working with store-bought lasagna sheets, cook for about 7 minutes, or according to package instructions.) Using a large spider, remove the sheets and lay them out on a lightly oiled surface (careful; they'll be hot). When cool enough to touch, unfurl the sheets and drizzle a little olive oil over them to keep them from sticking. Repeat with the remaining pasta sheets.

6   Butter a 9 by 13-inch baking dish, then spread with a thin layer of béchamel and Bolognese and cover with a layer of pasta. Add another layer of béchamel and Bolognese and a sprinkling of the Parmigiano and some pepper; then dot the top with tablespoons of ricotta. Repeat the layering until you have used all the ingredients, making sure to finish with béchamel, Parmigiano, and, finally, some basil. Cut the butter into small pieces and scatter on top.

7   Bake the lasagna until the top is golden and the edges are crisp, about 30 minutes. Let it rest and compose itself for about 10 minutes before cutting and serving.

—

TIPS

Bolognese can be made in advance, just reheat gently before assembling since it won't spend long in the oven.

If you don't have a food processor or blender, you can skip blending the sofrito-tomato mixture in Step 1; it will still be delicious.

You could also use beef short rib (see Beef Short Rib Pappardelle, page 220) for the meat filling instead of the Bolognese.

Superior Schnitzel

Makes 6 servings

—

3 or 4 skinless, boneless chicken breasts (about 2 pounds total)

¾ cup dark rye flour or all-purpose flour

2 large eggs

½ cup whole milk

1¾ to 2 cups sourdough bread crumbs (see page 69)

½ cup finely chopped mixed herbs, such as chives, oregano, parsley, or sage

½ cup extra-virgin olive oil, or as needed

Kosher salt

Freshly ground black pepper

Flaky sea salt

Lemon wedges for serving

—

TIP

It's easier to slice chicken breasts thinly when they're chilled and firm.

Flouring the schnitzel with dark rye flour and breading with sourdough bread crumbs and fresh herbs gives it a flavor upgrade. A chunky, thick schnitzel is not schnitzel, so make sure to slice and pound the meat as thinly as possible. Italians call this Milanese, and often add grated Parmigiano to the breading mix—something I sometimes do as well. Although this recipe uses chicken, both pork and veal work equally well. Schnitzel served with a creamy pasta is what I call a good night.

1   Lay a chicken breast on a cutting boarding and press the palm of your hand on top to secure it. Using a large, sharp knife, fillet the breast lengthwise into three equal cutlets about ¼ inch thick. Be careful not to slice your palm! Repeat with the remaining chicken.

2   Place the chicken cutlets between pieces of parchment paper and, using a mallet or rolling pin, pound gently until quite thin.

3   Get your schnitzel stations set up. Put the flour on a large plate. In a small bowl, beat together the eggs and milk for an egg wash. Put half the bread crumbs and all the herbs on a second large plate and stir together. (Replenish as needed.) Dust each chicken cutlet on both sides with flour, then dip into the egg wash, and press into the bread crumbs until well coated on both sides. Place the breaded schnitzels on a baking sheet in a single layer.

4   In a large skillet over medium-high heat, warm the olive oil until shimmering. Carefully place a couple of the schnitzels in the pan and cook until golden and crisp, a few minutes on both sides. Transfer the schnitzels to a second baking sheet, season with kosher salt and pepper, and keep warm in a low-temperature oven. Add more oil as needed between batches and continue cooking the remaining schnitzels.

5   Serve the schnitzels sprinkled with sea salt and lemon wedges on the side.

My Life in Schnitzel

1981: Learned to cook my first veal schnitzel with Aunty Deb.

1984–1998: Dodged precarious toothpicks in my nan's schnitzel saltimbocca.

1993: Traveled to Prague and had the biggest wiener schnitzel (sounds rude!) to date.

1995: My Croatian friend taught me that schnitzel can never be too thin.

1998: My grandfather taught me the old way of flouring and breading schnitzel on newspaper instead of plates. Makes for an easy cleanup.

1979–1983: Weekly shared a half-serving of schnitzel and spaghetti with my brother at our local Italian joint, the Trieste. Discovered pasta and schnitzel go together splendidly.

2015–present: Continue to make schnitzel and pasta for my family, whenever we need a pick-me-up.

1999: Cried when my local go-to Italian restaurant, the Aurora, closed. I was regularly tormented by prioritizing my budget and having to choose between the "schnitty" or the lasagna. Never fully recovered.

2008–2014: Ordered the schnitzel and creamy pasta at Prime Meats in Brooklyn every Sunday. Cried when they closed.

2014: Daily ate schnitzel Milanese on a trip to Bueno Aires, alongside some of the best homemade pasta in Argentina.

Sesame & Honey Panna Cotta

Makes 8 servings

—

½ cup untoasted white
sesame seeds

½ cup mild honey

3 tablespoons cold water

2½ teaspoons (¼-ounce packet)
unflavored gelatin

1 quart heavy cream

¼ cup granulated sugar

1 teaspoon vanilla extract

—

TIP

If you want to serve inverted
panna cotta, run a small knife
around the rim of the mold and
quickly dip the bottom into a bowl
of hot water. To help release it
from the sides, give the mold a
little shimmy, then carefully invert
it onto a dessert plate.

Swoon, sigh, swoon, sigh . . . I can't think of a nicer way
to end a meal than with a cool, light, jiggly panna cotta.
The subtle combination of sesame and honey is one of
my all-time favorites in a dessert. I've learned the hard
way—panna cotta is not a last-minute offering, so make
sure to allow enough time for chilling; or make it the
day before! I set and serve them in pretty champagne
coupes, petite glasses, or Jell-O molds so I don't have to
worry about inverting them.

1   In a small frying pan over low heat, gently toast the sesame seeds,
    stirring often, until fragrant and lightly golden, 3 to 4 minutes.

2   Transfer the sesame seeds in a mortar and pestle, add the honey,
    and then grind to make a smooth paste.

3   In a small bowl, combine the water and gelatin and stir to dissolve.
    Set aside.

4   In a large saucepan over low heat, combine the cream, sugar,
    and sesame-honey paste and bring to a simmer, gently letting the
    sesame infuse into the mixture, stirring occasionally, for about
    20 minutes. Don't let it boil.

5   Add the vanilla and gelatin to the warm cream mixture and whisk
    until completely dissolved.

6   Strain the mixture through a fine-mesh sieve into a large liquid mea-
    suring cup, then pour it into molds or your favorite small serving
    vessels.

7   Refrigerate the panna cotta, uncovered, until cool, then cover with
    plastic wrap and leave in the fridge until set, 3 to 4 hours but ideally
    overnight (depending on the size of your vessel), before serving.

Winter

It's time for oysters, wine-stained tablecloths, tortellini, earthy ceramics, an embarrassing excess of candles, and glassware, which may have come from another cabinet in another time. Wear something you love. Weekends should be spent with short rib ragù and pappardelle. Serve with a chunk of Parmigiano, chicory salad, and a big burly punch-you-in-the-face red. Take a pot of pasta e fagioli to a friend and feel good about life. Just so you know, the sausage-broccolini orecchiette works well with either sweet or spicy Italian sausage. Play around with different kinds of broccoli: broccolini, broccoli di spigariello, or Di Ciccio broccoli. Take a night walk. Come back and make gnocchi while in your socks. Have a bottle of sparkling Moscato d'Asti and a cheese plate for dessert if you don't have a blowtorch for crème brûlée. But trust me, splurge and get one; it's a game changer. Give your all to something you want, put on some old jewels or a tie, and spoon with someone—even if it's a pet. And remember, good company doesn't care about the clutter, the spoils, or a burst ravioli.

WINTER MENU

Preamble

Oysters with Peppercorn
& Fennel Mignonette

Sip

A Bone-Dry Prosecco Tower

Salad

Winter Chicories with Date & Anchovy Dressing

Pastas

Creamy Wild Mushroom & Potato Gnocchi

Carbonara

Gnocchi with Luxurious Pomodoro

Cannellini, Pancetta & Lemon Pasta e Fagioli

Crispy Italian Sausage & Broccolini Orecchiette

Classic Tortellini en Brodo

Cannelloni—Let's Bring It Back!

Beef Short Rib Pappardelle

"Damn, That's a Keeper" Winter Vegetable Lasagna

For a Feast

Skirt Steak with Olive Gremolata & Fried Gnocchi

Dessert

Gianduja Crème Brûlée

Oysters with Peppercorn & Fennel Mignonette

Makes 4 to 6 servings

—

Peppercorn & Fennel Mignonette

3 tablespoons very, very finely chopped fennel stalk

3 tablespoons very, very finely chopped red onion

½ teaspoon pink, white, or black peppercorns or a combination, crushed

⅓ cup champagne vinegar or red wine vinegar

¼ teaspoon fine sea salt or kosher salt

Coarse sea salt, or crushed ice

24 oysters in the shell, kept very cold

Fennel fronds for garnishing

Oysters whet the appetite and leave plenty of room for what's coming . . . pasta! I'm a sucker for petite, plump oysters, like buttery Sydney rock oysters and Pacific Northwest Kumamotos. If eating oysters "au naturel" is more your thing, I completely get it. However, here in California, wild, flowering fennel flanks the winding, treacherous coastal roads and was the inspiration for this pretty pink-and-green mignonette. The pink peppercorns add floral notes, the fennel stalk adds a little crunch, and the fronds do their thing, being all feathery and fabulous.

1   **To make the mignonette:** In a jar or small bowl, combine the chopped fennel, onion, crushed peppercorns, vinegar, and fine salt and shake or stir to mix. Cover and refrigerate for 15 minutes to lightly pickle and chill.

2   Pour some coarse sea salt or crushed ice onto a large serving platter (to stabilize the oysters), then carefully open the oysters and place on top, without losing any of their juices. Spoon a little mignonette into the pointy part of each oyster shell and garnish with a few delicate fennel fronds.

3   Serve the oysters with remainder of the mignonette to spoon on as desired.

To Shuck Oysters

An oyster is alive until you open it, so the sooner you eat it after shucking, the better. If the oyster smells suspicious, don't eat it. Heartbreaking, I know! Clean the oyster shells well under cold running water. Using a dish towel, grip the oyster, flat-side up, leaving the narrow, pointed tip, where the shells meet, exposed. Place the tip of the oyster knife where the top and bottom shells meet. Don't muscle it; you're looking for the sweet spot with your knife. Using your wrist, gently twist the knife, slowly prying the shell open. If you have difficulty, slightly adjust the position of the knife—like you're prying a key in a lock. Listen for the pop! Once the shell opens slightly, use the knife to work your way around the slit to detach the top from the bottom shell. Carefully run the knife under the flesh of the oyster to detach it from the bottom shell. Throughout the process, make sure not to lose a drop of the precious briny juice.

A Bone-Dry Prosecco Tower

Makes one 7-coupe tower

—

One 750ml bottle brut-style
Prosecco, chilled

—

TIPS

You'll use one 750ml bottle for
seven coupes; please do the math
if you want to scale up.

Try adding a slice of blood orange
to each filled glass of bubbles.
It's a simple winter-citrus garnish
that adds a whimsical watercolor-
like hue to the liquor. Alternatively,
in the warmer months, pop in an
edible flower to pretty things up.

Lead me to an overflowing tower of bubbles. I want a conga line, elaborate synchronized swimming routines, lipstick, and sequins. During lockdown, I became obsessed with vintage coupes and champagne towers. I think I was drawn to the Gatsby-like escapism they evoke. Apparently, they became popular at speakeasies in America during Prohibition. Everything felt off-limits during lockdown, so I'm not surprised that I started building them during this period. I highly encourage you to call a few friends and get ambitious on the build, but even a modest tower for two can lift the spirits. If you don't find any etched coupes in a dusty family cabinet, just know that I bought mine on Etsy. Instead of Champagne, I'm using Prosecco from Italy's northeast and is known for its fruit character. There are different levels of dryness, but I like it very dry—like bone-dry—which is often labeled "extra brut." Ask your local wine store for a Prosecco that's been aged longer, which results in a slightly more complex character.

1   Find a solid, flat base on which to build your tower. (Place a tray underneath the glasses if you want to catch the overflow; and have a straw at the ready.)

2   Place four coupes on the base. The most important part is to make sure that each glass touches the surrounding glasses. There should be a diamond-shape gap between each glass; these are where the bubbles will travel down. Center the stems of two coupes over the diamond openings that were created by the layer below. Top the second layer with a seventh coupe. (Larger towers are made of successively smaller layers of squares. If the bottom layer has five by five coupes, the layer above will have four by four coupes, and so on. For large or small towers, repeat the layers until there is a single coupe on top.)

3   Once assembled, begin to slowly pour the Prosecco into the top coupe and laugh your head off with delight as the Prosecco begins to trickle downward. If the coupes do not fill entirely, just top them off individually. Or if you don't want to waste a drop of bubbly, I totally get it. Simply fill each coupe separately and enjoy the sculptural beauty.

Winter Chicories with Date & Anchovy Dressing

Makes 4 servings

—

5 to 6 cups mixed winter chicories
3 anchovies, finely chopped
1 garlic clove, finely grated
¼ teaspoon kosher salt
2 tablespoons lemon juice
2 teaspoons champagne vinegar or sherry vinegar
2 teaspoons date molasses, brown sugar, honey, or maple syrup
¼ cup extra-virgin olive oil
Freshly ground black pepper

—

TIP

If you don't have date molasses but are lucky enough to have small, soft Barhi dates that taste like caramel, substitute 2 finely chopped dates for the 2 teaspoons date molasses.

I'm captivated by winter chicories; Tardivo and Treviso—with their tangled, tightly bundled, elongated leaves—are varieties that look like sea creatures. Castelfranco radicchio, with its delicate pink-flecked leaves, looks painterly, like a bouquet of peonies. The bold salty-sweet dressing and bitter chicories are flavor heavyweights; they stand up to and complement one another in this simple striking salad.

1   In cool water, wash the chicories, dry thoroughly in a clean dish towel or salad spinner, and then arrange in a large serving bowl.

2   In a mortar and pestle (or using the side of a large knife and a cutting board), mash the anchovies, garlic, and salt until they become a thick paste. Add the lemon juice, vinegar, and molasses and stir to combine. Slowly whisk in the olive oil.

3   Toss the chicories with the anchovy dressing, and finish with some cranks of pepper just before serving.

Creamy Wild Mushroom & Potato Gnocchi

Makes 4 servings

Fresh pasta: 1 recipe Potato Gnocchi (page 25)

Store-bought pasta: 1½ to 1¾ pounds potato gnocchi

—

4 tablespoons extra-virgin olive oil, or as needed

1 pound mixed mushrooms (such as baby shiitakes, oyster, and cremini), large ones torn into bite-size pieces, plus more for garnishing

1 shallot, finely diced

1 garlic clove, finely diced

¾ cup chicken stock

2 teaspoons fresh thyme, plus more for garnishing

½ cup sour cream

2 tablespoons unsalted butter, at room temperature

½ teaspoon kosher salt

Freshly ground black pepper

Finely grated Parmigiano-Reggiano for sprinkling

—

TIP

Moisture is the enemy of crisp mushrooms. Don't soak or rinse fresh mushrooms under water as they will absorb too much liquid. Instead, wipe them clean with a damp paper towel or clean dish towel.

Soft potato gnocchi and crispy mushrooms tossed in a creamy sauce will warm the cockles on a cool night. If stinky cheese is your thing, you might want to melt a knob or two in the creamy sauce.

1   Bring a large pot of lightly salted water to a boil.

2   In a large heavy-bottomed frying pan or skillet over medium-high heat, warm 2 tablespoons of the olive oil. Add half the mushrooms and cook, tossing occasionally, until tender but crisp, 5 to 7 minutes. Remove the mushrooms from the pan and transfer to a plate. Repeat with the remaining 2 tablespoons olive oil and mushrooms. Keep warm.

3   Turn the heat to medium-low, add another splash of olive oil, if the pan is dry, add the shallot and garlic, and sauté until translucent and soft, about 2 minutes.

4   Add the chicken stock to the pan and deglaze, scraping up the browned bits with a wooden spoon. Add the thyme, turn the heat to low, and reduce the stock by half. Stir in the sour cream and let simmer gently.

5   Add half the gnocchi to the boiling water and cook for 2 to 3 minutes, or according to package instructions if using store-bought. When they float to the surface, it's a good indication they're done. Pop one in your mouth to make sure it's cooked through. Using a slotted spoon, transfer the cooked gnocchi into the frying pan. Repeat with the remaining gnocchi.

6   Stir ½ cup of the gnocchi water into the pan and toss to coat. Return most of the mushrooms to the pan along with the butter and gently toss to combine. Season with the salt and pepper.

7   Serve the gnocchi sprinkled with Parmigiano and garnished with the reserved mushrooms and some thyme.

Carbonara

Makes 2 servings

Fresh pasta: ½ recipe Simple Semolina Dough (page 27), shaped into pici (see page 50)

Store-bought pasta: 8 ounces dried bucatini or spaghetti

—

3 tablespoons extra-virgin olive oil

4 ounces guanciale (with skin removed), pancetta, or thick-cut bacon, diced into ¼-inch cubes

2 garlic cloves, smashed

Freshly ground black pepper

2 egg yolks, at room temperature

1 cup finely grated Pecorino Romano, plus more for serving

½ teaspoon kosher salt

—

TIPS

I find that carbonara is easier to execute with a smaller quantity of pasta; this is why the recipe serves just two (generously). But it can be doubled.

Use a frying pan with deep sides; it'll give the pasta plenty of room when it's tossed.

Carbonara is about creating an emulsion; combining fat with water for a creamy sauce. Adding the eggs *off the heat,* while continuously stirring or tossing, helps prevent them from getting too hot and scrambling.

Don't rely on pre-grated cheese here; grate your own, finely, using a Microplane or the finest side of a box grater.

I've had a long and complicated relationship with carbonara. I've committed all sorts of crimes against it. When I was thirteen, I made a version using béchamel sauce; way too thick and stodgy. By my late teens, I had graduated to using heavy cream—a lighter affair than the béchamel—an improvement but not an egg in sight. And I still hadn't worked out the correct ratio of pasta to sauce. Eventually, I learned how to emulsify eggs, pork fat, cheese, and pasta water to create a creamy coating on the sturdy pasta. But here's my truth, and it might be controversial: Sometimes I find carbonara too eggy. My version doesn't go crazy on the eggs, and hopefully alleviates any fear of scrambling them. To compensate, I add a little more oil and infuse it with garlic. Okay, okay . . . even now, I'm not doing the "right" thing by this Roman classic, but at the end of the day, everyone finds their own carbonara.

1   In a frying pan over low heat, warm the olive oil. Add the guanciale, garlic, and some cranks of pepper and sauté, stirring often, until the guanciale has rendered its fat and is crisp, 6 to 8 minutes. Remove from the heat, discard the garlic, transfer the crispy meat to a plate, and set aside. Keep the oil in the pan.

2   Meanwhile, bring a large pot of lightly salted water to a boil. Add the pasta and cook until al dente, about 4 minutes or a minute or two shy of the package instructions if using store-bought.

3   While the pasta is cooking, in a small bowl, whisk together the egg yolks and a splash of pasta water to temper them, then mix in the pecorino, salt, and more generous cranks of pepper.

4   Using a large spider or tongs, transfer the pasta straight into the frying pan with the reserved guanciale-garlic oil; toss well. Be sure to reserve the pasta water; this is crucial.

5   Off the heat, add ½ cup of the pasta water to the pasta and then the egg-cheese mixture, continuously stirring and tossing (just keep the pasta moving).

6   Return the pan to medium-low heat, then add another ½ cup pasta water while continuing to toss, toss, toss or stir, stir, stir until the pasta water has been absorbed and a luscious creamy sauce coats the pasta, about 3 minutes.

7   Serve the pasta topped with the crispy guanciale and more pepper and pecorino.

Gnocchi with Luxurious Pomodoro

Makes 4 servings

Fresh pasta: 1 recipe Potato Gnocchi (page 25)

Store-bought pasta: 1½ to 1¾ pounds potato gnocchi

—

1 recipe Luxurious Pomodoro in a Flash (page 59), warm

Finely grated Pecorino Romano or Parmigiano-Reggiano for serving

Freshly ground black pepper

I had my first bowl of potato gnocchi at Old Papa's Cafe in Fremantle, Western Australia. This port town was a hub for many Italians seeking a new beginning after World War II. The café was opened in the late 1960s by a Sicilian-born emigrant who re-created the Italian alfresco street cafés of his childhood. What started as a dingy dive, where patrons gambled and sat ringside watching the occasional boxing match, turned into a beloved institution. Italians owned and ran delicatessens, greengrocers, butchers, and barbershops throughout Freo. I was a pimply teenager when we moved to the isolated west coast and I lapped up the freedom this small village enabled. When we weren't trying to sneak into the pubs, underage, I used to meet my friends for pasta or coffee at Old Papa's. On the blisteringly hot summer nights, they served ice-cold lemon granita that quenched our thirst while we waited for the cooling sea breeze, known as the Fremantle Doctor, to arrive. But back to the gnocchi. I can still vividly recall that very first bite. Even in the dead of summer, it hit the spot, served with a simple tomato sauce (as pictured) in a hand-painted Maiolica ceramic bowl. Each table had a generous serving of grated pecorino that you could keep adding, which I did again and again, before I mourned the last gnocchi. If I can get you to make just *one thing* in this book, it is this recipe—it's so simple. You'll never tire of it. In fact, I'm betting it will become a dinner staple.

1   Bring a large pot of lightly salted water to a boil. Add half the gnocchi and cook for 2 to 3 minutes, or according to package instructions if using store-bought. When they float to the surface, it's a good indication they're done. Pop one in your mouth to make sure it's cooked through. Using a slotted spoon, transfer the cooked gnocchi into the warm sauce. Repeat with the remaining gnocchi.

2   Serve the gnocchi with lots of pecorino and pepper.

Cannellini, Pancetta & Lemon Pasta e Fagioli

Makes 6 servings

Store-bought pasta: 4 ounces any small dried pasta, such as rotelle no. 54, small shells, or ditalini

—

3 tablespoons extra-virgin olive oil

6 ounces pancetta, diced

2 bunches (about 1 pound) rainbow chard or spinach, stems trimmed and finely chopped, leaves coarsely chopped

2 yellow onions, finely diced

4 celery stalks, finely chopped

2 carrots, finely chopped

6 garlic cloves, finely chopped

8 sprigs thyme, stemmed

2 bay leaves

1¼ teaspoons kosher salt

Freshly ground black pepper

2 quarts chicken stock

Two 15-ounce cans cannellini beans, drained and rinsed

1 Parmigiano-Reggiano rind (optional), plus finely grated Parmigiano-Reggiano for sprinkling

Juice of 2 lemons

The first time that I traveled to Florence, I ordered a soup at a restaurant near the Piazza del Duomo that was possibly the best soup I've ever had in my life. It was a cross between pasta e fagioli and minestrone. On the train ride to Siena, I seriously contemplated doubling back to experience it one more time. I'm not kidding. I've been trying to re-create that soup ever since with pancetta, cannellini beans, vegetables, chicken stock, Parmigiano-Reggiano rind, and lots of lemon. Serve this humble, soul-warming soup with garlic bread (see page 70) or a crusty baguette.

1   In a Dutch oven or large heavy-bottomed saucepan over low heat, warm the olive oil. Add the pancetta and sauté until lightly browned, about 5 minutes. Stir in the chard stems, onions, celery, carrots, garlic, thyme, and bay leaves and season with the salt and pepper. Cook gently, stirring often, until softened but not brown, 12 to 15 minutes.

2   Turn the heat to medium and add the chicken stock, beans, pasta, and Parmigiano rind (if using) to the pan. Bring to a simmer, stirring occasionally, and cook until the pasta is just al dente (likely a bit longer than the package instructions because you're simmering, not boiling, in the stock).

3   Discard the bay leaves and Parmigiano rind. Stir in the chard leaves until they've wilted. Add the lemon juice and adjust the seasoning if needed.

4   Serve the pasta hot and steamy with a sprinkling of more Parmigiano.

Crispy Italian Sausage & Broccolini Orecchiette

Makes 4 servings

Fresh pasta: 1 recipe Simple Semolina Dough (page 27), shaped into orecchiette (see page 49)

Store-bought pasta: 14 ounces dried orecchiette or cavatelli

—

1 bunch (about 10 ounces) broccolini

¼ cup extra-virgin olive oil

1 shallot, finely chopped

3 garlic cloves, finely chopped

3 links (12 to 14 ounces) sweet or hot Italian sausage, casings removed

¾ cup chopped flat leaf parsley

½ teaspoon kosher salt

Freshly ground black pepper

2 tablespoons unsalted butter

⅓ cup grated Parmigiano-Reggiano, plus more for topping

¼ to ½ teaspoon red pepper flakes

—

TIP

A farmer taught me that broccolini are sweeter during the cooler months, when they produce more sugar to protect themselves from frost. If you see purple tips on the leaves, it's a sign you're on to a good thing. Keep an eye out for leafy broccoli rabe, also known as rapini, or an Italian heirloom variety called Di Ciccio.

The first dinner that I had with my editor, Kelly, was at Frankies 457 Spuntino, a Brooklyn institution. It was my local Italian restaurant for over a decade. Frankies' house-made pastas are so ridiculously good it's torture having to decide what to order. That evening, we both ended up having cavatelli with sausage (perhaps sowing the seeds for *Simple Pasta* before we even knew it). Homemade orecchiette is so charming that it deserves a simple, tasty sauce such as this. Sometimes I add a whole, fresh pepperoncini chile along with the shallot for a hit of sweet heat. This one is for Kelly, who speaks the same food language as I do.

1   Bring two large pots of lightly salted water to a boil.

2   Trim the broccolini and slice the stems into ½-inch pieces, leaving at least 1 inch of the stem on every floret. Add the broccolini stems and florets to one of the pots of boiling water and blanch until crisp-tender, 2 to 3 minutes. Drain in a colander and set aside.

3   In a large frying pan over medium-low heat, warm the olive oil. Add the shallot and garlic and sauté for a couple of minutes. Add the sausage, turn the heat to medium-high, and cook, breaking it up into small pieces with a wooden spoon, until it's deliciously brown and crisp, 12 to 15 minutes. Then add the broccolini and parsley, season with the salt and pepper, and stir to combine. Keep warm.

4   Add the orecchiette to the second pot of boiling water and cook for 3 to 4 minutes, or according to package instructions if using store-bought. Using a large spider or slotted spoon, transfer the pasta into the sausage mixture along with the butter, Parmigiano, and ¼ cup of the pasta water and toss to combine.

5   Serve the pasta topped with more Parmigiano and the red pepper flakes.

Classic Tortellini en Brodo

Makes 6 servings

Fresh pasta: 1 recipe Large-Batch Egg Dough (page 16), prepared through Step 2

Store-bought pasta: Three 12-ounce packages of meat-filled tortellini (if using store-bought tortellini, either make your own brodo or buy a really great broth)

Review the techniques for filling pasta (see page 34) and shaping pasta (see page 37) before starting the recipe.

—

Brodo

2 pounds chicken bones

1 pound pork bones

1 large yellow onion, halved

1 unpeeled garlic head, halved

½ fennel bulb, chopped

3 celery stalks, chopped

2 carrots, chopped

2 bay leaves

1 Parmigiano-Reggiano rind

1 teaspoon black peppercorns

5½ quarts cold water

Filling

5 ounces boneless pork shoulder

½ teaspoon kosher salt

3 tablespoons unsalted butter

1 tablespoon extra-virgin olive oil

1 sprig rosemary

¾ cup dry white wine

3 ounces prosciutto, coarsely chopped

3 ounces mortadella (without nuts), coarsely chopped

1½ cups finely grated Parmigiano-Reggiano, plus more for serving

1 large egg

½ teaspoon lemon zest

⅛ teaspoon freshly grated nutmeg

I promise that you'll squeal with delight when you successfully shape your first tortellini. I tinkered around with this classic, altering both the filling and the brodo (Italian for "broth"), trying to save you time, but what I discovered is that classics are *classics* for a reason. Your reward comes with the love and time you put in, not with shortcuts. Learning to make brodo and shape tortellini is a life skill, and you will be so stinkin' proud of yourself for nailing this one. I make the flavorful brodo the day before, giving it plenty of time to gently extract as much flavor as possible from the bones, veggies, and aromatics. While that's simmering, I prepare the filling and keep it in an airtight container in the fridge overnight. The following day, when I plan to serve them, I make the pasta dough, then fill and shape the plump tortellini. This way, the pasta feels manageable, relaxed, and full of love and attention. Contrary to the stated yield, my family of four can take these all down—we have big appetites!

1   **To make the brodo:** Rinse the chicken and pork bones under cold running water.

2   In a large deep pot or Dutch oven over medium-high heat, combine the bones, onion, garlic, fennel, celery, carrots, bay leaves, Parmigiano rind, peppercorns, and 5½ quarts water. Bring to a gentle boil, then turn the heat to low and let simmer. Try not to stir or disturb it as it simmers but skim off the impurities and fat as needed. Continue to simmer very gently, so the brodo doesn't evaporate too much, for 4 to 5 hours. Remove from the heat, discard the bones and vegetables, and then strain through a fine-mesh sieve. Return the brodo to the pot; this is what you'll cook your tortellini in.

3   **To make the filling:** Season the pork with the salt.

Continued

Classic Tortellini en Brodo, continued

4   In a frying pan over medium heat, melt together the butter and olive oil. Add the rosemary and pork and sear until lightly browned on all sides, about 5 minutes total. Turn the heat to low, add the wine, and let the pork simmer, basting and rotating, until it's tender and cooked through, about 6 minutes more (add a splash of brodo if the liquid evaporates too quickly). Remove the pan from the heat, discard the rosemary, and coarsely chop the pork.

5   Transfer the chopped pork and a few tablespoons of the meaty juices into a food processor and pulse a few times. Then add the chopped prosciutto and mortadella and pulse until finely ground. Add the Parmigiano, egg, lemon zest, and nutmeg and pulse just until combined into a sticky paste. If not using immediately, store, covered, in the fridge.

6   If using fresh pasta, roll out the dough, then cut, fill, and shape into tortellini. Place, uncovered, on the prepared baking sheet, making sure they aren't touching.

7   Bring the brodo to a gentle boil over medium heat. Add half the tortellini and cook, stirring occasionally, for 3 to 4 minutes, or according to package instructions if using store-bought. Taste one to see if it's done. Using a large spider or slotted spoon, transfer the cooked tortellini into individual bowls. Repeat with the remaining tortellini.

8   Once all the tortellini are cooked, add a ladleful of the warm brodo to each bowl. Serve pronto with additional Parmigiano on the side.

—

TIPS

For the brodo, use gelatinous bones to extract a rich flavor and achieve a glassy finish. If making the brodo in advance, let cool and refrigerate it; then skim and discard any solids before reheating. If you are short on time or feel your brodo is lacking depth of flavor, lightly season with salt or—I won't tell anyone—add some bouillon. Just keep in mind the filling in the tortellini is salty.

These tortellini are equally delicious, and quicker, served with brown butter and sage.

Cannelloni—
Let's Bring It Back!

Makes 6 to 8 servings

Fresh pasta: ½ recipe Large-Batch Egg Dough (page 16) to make approximately twelve 7-inch cannelloni (see page 31)

Store-bought pasta: Approximately twenty-eight 4-inch cannelloni or manicotti shells

—

Filling

½ cup extra-virgin olive oil, or as needed

2 bunches (about 1 pound) Swiss chard or spinach, stems trimmed and finely diced, leaves finely chopped

2 leeks, white and light green parts only, washed and thinly sliced

2 shallots, finely diced

5 garlic cloves, finely diced

1 teaspoon kosher salt

½ cup chopped mint

⅔ cup chopped basil leaves

24 ounces whole-milk ricotta

1 cup finely grated Parmigiano-Reggiano

1 large egg

1 tablespoon lemon zest

Freshly ground black pepper

Cannelloni Béchamel

3 tablespoons unsalted butter

3 tablespoons all-purpose flour

1¾ cups whole milk, warmed

½ cup finely grated Parmigiano-Reggiano

½ teaspoon kosher salt

⅛ teaspoon ground nutmeg

Freshly ground black pepper

Cannelloni feels a little 1980s to some, but I'm crazy for it and I think it's time it had a comeback. This is a great vegetarian pasta, packed full of leeks, mint, and basil and plenty of fresh ricotta. You'll feel nourished just looking at your cutting board overflowing with glorious greens. None of the components are complicated, but cannelloni (similar to lasagna) is a perfect example of *simple* not always being *fast*, so save it for the weekend. To be honest, sometimes I use a good store-bought red sauce to save a little time, but Mama Sordo's Red Sauce would make it the real deal. Cannelloni is perfect for feeding a crowd on a cold, cozy night.

1   **To make the filling:** In a large frying pan over medium heat, warm the olive oil. Add the chard stems, leeks, shallots, garlic, and salt and sauté, stirring often, until softened, about 8 minutes. Add the chard leaves and let wilt. Remove from the heat and stir in the mint and basil; set aside to cool.

2   In a large bowl, combine the ricotta, Parmigiano, egg, lemon zest, and generous cranks of pepper. Stir in the cooled chard-leek mixture. Set aside.

3   **To make the béchamel:** In a large heavy-bottomed saucepan over low heat, melt the butter. Add the flour and cook for 2 minutes, whisking constantly. Gradually whisk in the milk until smooth. When the béchamel has the consistency of heavy cream, whisk in the Parmigiano, salt, nutmeg, and some pepper. Set aside.

4   If using fresh pasta, divide the dough in half, then roll out both sheets to #6. Lay both sheets on a lightly floured surface and cut into approximately twelve 6 by 7-inch rectangles.

Continued

Cannelloni—Let's Bring It Back!, continued

1 recipe Mama Sordo's Red Sauce (page 58), or 3 cups store-bought tomato sauce

Grated Parmigiano-Reggiano for sprinkling

—

TIP

Prepare and assemble the cannelloni a day ahead, cover, and refrigerate. Before baking, refresh with a sprinkling of cheese and a splash of olive oil.

5   Bring a large pot of lightly salted water to a boil. Working in batches, add the pasta and blanch until just softened, 1 to 2 minutes, or cook according to package instructions if using store-bought. Using a large spider, remove the sheets and lay them out on a clean surface. (Careful, they'll be hot!) When cool enough to touch, unfurl the sheets and splash a little olive oil over them to stop them from sticking.

6   *If working with fresh pasta:* Using a piping bag or spoon, make a 2-inch-thick rope of filling along the length of each rectangle, about 1 inch from the bottom. Roll the pasta up and over the filling, like a log, to form each cannelloni.

If working with dried pasta: Stuff the cannelloni shells with the filling.

7   Spread the red sauce evenly across the bottoms of two 9 by 12-inch baking dishes. Nestle the cannelloni, seam-side down, on the sauce. Spoon the béchamel on top of each cannelloni. (If you will be baking later, cover and refrigerate.)

8   Preheat the oven to 350°F.

9   Sprinkle the cannelloni with Parmigiano (add a little butter or olive oil to any exposed pasta edges). Bake for 25 to 30 minutes, if using fresh pasta, or 30 to 35 minutes or according to package instructions, if using store-bought. Finally, crisp up the edges by placing the baking dishes under a broiler for a minute or two. Just don't get distracted and burn your masterpiece!

10 Serve the cannelloni in the baking dishes, making sure to use clean dish towels to cover the hot handles so no one burns themselves.

Beef Short Rib Pappardelle

Makes 6 servings

Fresh pasta: 1 recipe Large-Batch Egg Dough (page 16), cut into pappardelle (see page 31)

Store-bought pasta: 1 pound dried pappardelle

—

3 pounds bone-in beef short ribs, 4 to 5 inches long

Kosher salt

Freshly ground black pepper

3 tablespoons extra-virgin olive oil, or as needed

1 large yellow onion, finely diced

2 celery stalks, finely diced

3 carrots, finely diced

5 garlic cloves, finely diced

2 tablespoons tomato paste

1 teaspoon red pepper flakes

1 bay leaf

¼ cup red wine vinegar

½ cup full-bodied red wine

One 28-ounce can San Marzano crushed tomatoes

3 cups beef broth, or as needed

2 sprigs thyme

2 sprigs sage

2 sprigs oregano, plus leaves for sprinkling

Crème fraîche for serving (optional)

Finely grated Parmigiano-Reggiano for serving

—

TIPS

Look for beef short ribs that are nicely marbled but not too fatty.

The ragù can be made a day or two ahead and reheated before serving. Skim off any fat that may have formed before reheating.

Ribbons of pappardelle, melt-in-your-mouth short rib ragù, and a swirl of crème fraîche will make you feel as if you're dining by a crackling fire. I build the braise off the back of the mother of canned tomatoes, San Marzano (pick up the Italian-grown D.O.P. kind if you can); good stock (grab from the butcher when you get the ribs if you don't have some at home); and red wine vinegar (to give the ragù some zing). Get a big, juicy Australian or Californian "Cab Sav" both for braising and sipping while this dish slowly cooks.

1   Preheat the oven to 325°F.

2   Generously season the short ribs with salt and pepper.

3   In a large Dutch oven over medium-high heat, warm the olive oil. When it's shimmering, add the short ribs, working in batches so as not to crowd the pan, and brown on all sides, 8 to 10 minutes total. Remove the browned ribs from the pot and transfer to a large bowl. Set aside.

4   Turn the heat to medium; add the onion, celery, and carrots to the pot; and cook, stirring occasionally, until soft and golden, 10 to 15 minutes.

5   Stir the garlic, tomato paste, red pepper flakes, and bay leaf into the vegetables and sauté for 1 minute. Add the vinegar and wine and let simmer for a couple of minutes, scraping up any browned bits with a wooden spoon.

6   Add the tomatoes, beef broth, and herb sprigs to the pot; return the browned beef ribs; and bring to a simmer.

7   Cover the pot and place it in the oven. Cook until the ribs are very tender, 2½ to 3 hours; basting and turning the meat occasionally, and adding more broth or water if needed to make sure the ribs are partially submerged in liquid as they cook.

8   Remove the pot from the oven, skim off the excess fat from the surface, and discard the bay leaf and any herb stems. Transfer the ribs to a cutting board. When they are cool enough to handle, trim off any fatty pieces, then remove the meat from the bones and use a fork to shred it. Return the meat to the sauce and keep warm.

9   Bring a large pot of lightly salted water to a boil. Add the pasta and cook until al dente, 3 to 4 minutes or according to package instructions if using store-bought. Drain in a colander, then return the pasta to the pot and splash a little olive oil on it to keep it from sticking.

10   Serve the pasta with the ragù, a dollop of crème fraîche, and sprinkling of Parmigiano and oregano leaves.

"Damn, That's a Keeper" Winter Vegetable Lasagna

Makes 8 to 10 servings

Fresh pasta: 1 recipe Large-Batch Egg Dough (page 16), cut into lasagna sheets (see page 31) that fit a 9 by 13-inch baking dish

Store-bought pasta: Approximately 12 ounces dried lasagna sheets

—

1 large butternut squash (about 3 pounds), peeled, seeded, and cut into ¼-inch slices

½ cup extra-virgin olive oil, or as needed

Kosher salt

Freshly ground black pepper

8 tablespoons unsalted butter, or as needed

4 tablespoons water

6 garlic cloves

1 small cauliflower (about 1¼ pounds), cut into ¼-inch slices

2 fennel bulbs (about 1½ pounds total), thinly sliced

This is a sublime, elegant, winter-vegetable lasagna. I'm not going to lie—it's a time commitment; but I guarantee that once you've made this, it will become one of your go-to special meals. No awkward chunks of vegetables here, friends, just thin slivers of squash, cauliflower, and fennel layered between thin sheets of pasta, pesto, creamy béchamel, and Parmigiano-Reggiano. I give the vegetables the royal treatment by basting them in garlic butter, a method that I learned from a friend, who learned it from his father, who learned it from Marcella Hazan (many roads lead back to Marcella). Instead of red wine, why not serve this with an herbaceous bottle of Sauvignon Blanc, which keeps this white-sauced lasagna wonderful and light.

1   Preheat the oven to 350°F. Line two large baking sheets with parchment paper.

2   Toss the squash in ¼ cup of the olive oil, season with salt and pepper, and spread out evenly in a single layer on the prepared baking sheets. Scatter 2 tablespoons of the butter and 2 tablespoons of the water on each sheet, cover tightly with aluminum foil, and cook until softened, about 15 minutes, then remove from the oven. Set aside.

3   While the squash is cooking, in a large frying pan over medium-high heat, warm 2 tablespoons butter and 2 tablespoons olive oil with 3 garlic cloves. Working in batches if needed, add the cauliflower, season with a little salt, and sauté, basting with the garlic-infused butter. Try not to break up the delicate slices (adding more butter and olive oil as needed). Cook until tender, about 15 minutes. Remove everything from the pan and set aside.

Continued

**"Damn, That's a Keeper"
Winter Vegetable Lasagna,
continued**

Creamy Béchamel

6 tablespoons unsalted butter

⅓ cup all-purpose flour

3¾ cups whole milk, warmed

6 sautéed garlic cloves
(reserved from the squash)

1 cup finely grated
Parmigiano-Reggiano

2 teaspoons kosher salt

⅛ teaspoon ground nutmeg

Freshly ground white or
black pepper

1½ cups finely grated
Parmigiano-Reggiano

1 cup Cavolo Nero, Parmigiano
& Pistachio Pesto (page 63)
or store-bought basil pesto

Freshly ground white or
black pepper

Basil leaves for finishing

3 tablespoons unsalted butter,
cut into small pieces

Flaky sea salt

—

TIP

Use two large frying pans to
sauté the cauliflower and fennel
simultaneously. The vegetables
can also be prepped and cooked
the day before.

4   Add the remaining 2 tablespoons butter, remaining 2 tablespoons olive oil, and remaining 3 garlic cloves to the same pan. Working in batches if needed, add the fennel and season with a little salt. Sauté until soft and caramelized, 15 to 20 minutes (adding more butter and oil as needed). Turn off the heat and remove all the garlic from both the fennel and cauliflower. Finely chop the garlic and set aside.

5   **To make the béchamel:** In a large heavy-bottomed saucepan over low heat, melt the butter. Add the flour and cook for 2 minutes while constantly whisking. Gradually whisk in the milk, until smooth. When the béchamel has the consistency of heavy cream, whisk in the chopped garlic, Parmigiano, salt, nutmeg, and some cranks of pepper to combine.

6   Bring a large pot of lightly salted water to a boil. Working in batches, add four sheets of pasta at a time and blanch just until softened, 1 to 2 minutes, or cook for 7 to 8 minutes or according to package instructions if using store-bought. Using a large spider, remove the sheets and lay them out on a clean surface. (Careful, they'll be hot!) When cool enough to touch, unfurl the sheets and splash a little olive oil over them to keep them from sticking. Repeat with the remaining pasta sheets.

7   Preheat the oven to 400°F.

8   Butter a deep 9 by 13-inch baking dish, spread a thin layer of béchamel over the bottom, cover with a layer of pasta, then add a layer of squash. Sprinkle some of the fennel and Parmigiano on top, dot with a little pesto, and season with pepper. Cover with another layer of pasta, béchamel, and now cauliflower. Sprinkle more fennel and Parmigiano on top and add a little more pesto and pepper. Finish with a layer of squash, since you'll still have some left, then a final layer of pasta, béchamel, Parmigiano, and basil. Scatter the butter pieces on top.

9   Bake the lasagna until the top is golden and the edges are crisp, about 30 minutes. Let it rest and compose itself for about 10 minutes and sprinkle with sea salt just before serving.

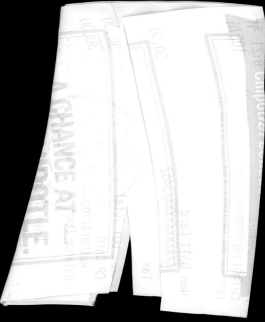

Skirt Steak with Olive Gremolata & Fried Gnocchi

Makes 4 servings

Fresh pasta: 1 recipe Potato Gnocchi (page 25)

Store-bought pasta: 1½ to 1¾ pounds gnocchi

—

Extra-virgin olive oil for drizzling, plus 3 tablespoons, or as needed

4 tablespoons unsalted butter, or as needed

½ teaspoon kosher salt

Finely grated Parmigiano-Reggiano for sprinkling

Olive Gremolata

1 large garlic clove, finely chopped

1½ cups finely chopped flat-leaf parsley

½ cup finely chopped pitted green olives

½ cup extra-virgin olive oil

3 tablespoons red wine vinegar

1 tablespoon lemon zest, plus 1 tablespoon lemon juice

Freshly ground black pepper

1 pound skirt steak

Kosher salt

Freshly ground black pepper

Extra-virgin olive oil for drizzling

I've got a thing for skirt steak. It's full of flavor, forgiving, and it cooks in no time. My favorite way to have it is with potato gnocchi *that's been fried.* Yes, you heard that right. It's my play on steak frites. Your world feels right when the steak's juices marry with the crispy gnocchi and the olive-herb gremolata. It feels even more complete after uncorking a bottle of Brunello. Just remember to leave room for Gianduja Crème Brûlée (page 229) . . . invite me over!

1   In a large bowl, combine equal parts water and ice cubes to prepare an ice bath.

2   Bring a large pot of lightly salted water to a boil. Working in two batches, cook the gnocchi for about 2 minutes, or according to package instructions if using store-bought. When the gnocchi float to the surface, it's a good indication they're done. Pop one in your mouth to make sure it's cooked through. Using a slotted spoon, transfer the gnocchi to the ice bath for a quick dip to stop them from cooking and remove the gummy exterior. Strain well, transfer to a large baking sheet, and toss with a drizzle of olive oil to lightly coat.

3   Line a plate with a layer of paper towels. In a large cast-iron skillet over medium-high heat, melt together the butter and 3 tablespoons olive oil. Working in a few batches, add the gnocchi and fry until golden and crisp on all sides, about 2 minutes, adding more butter or oil as needed. Transfer the gnocchi to the prepared plate, season with the salt, and top with a generous sprinkling of Parmigiano. Keep warm.

4   **To make the gremolata:** In a small bowl, combine the garlic, parsley, olives, olive oil, vinegar, lemon zest, lemon juice, and some cranks of pepper and stir to incorporate. Set aside.

5   Pat the steak dry with paper towels, then generously season on both sides with salt and pepper. If the steak is too long to fit in your largest cast-iron skillet, cut it to fit.

TIP

I'll fire up two skillets to accommodate 1 pound of steak. If you don't feel like cleaning the stove top afterward, cook the steak in a 400°F oven until an instant-read thermometer reaches 130°F, about 18 minutes. In the summer, I cook the steak on an oiled grill.

6   Set the cast-iron skillet (or two skillets) over high heat for about 5 minutes to get very hot. Add a drizzle of olive oil to the skillet(s) and immediately add the steak. Let cook, undisturbed, until the bottom is seared and brown, 4 to 5 minutes, then flip and continue cooking until an instant-read thermometer reaches 130°F for medium-rare; or 140°F for medium, 2 to 3 minutes more. Transfer the steak to a cutting board and let it rest for about 5 minutes before cutting against the grain into ½-inch-thick slices.

7   Place the steak on a platter and pour any juices left on the cutting board over it. Serve with the gremolata and fried gnocchi.

Gianduja Crème Brûlée

Makes 8 servings

—

3 cups heavy cream

2 large eggs, plus 4 egg yolks

½ cup granulated sugar, plus 16 teaspoons

¼ teaspoon kosher salt

½ cup Italian hazelnut-chocolate spread (such as Nocciolata)

2 teaspoons vanilla extract

I'm completely smitten by the flavor combination of hazelnut and chocolate. When I first went to Italy, I had a scoop of gianduja gelato every day. This crème brûlée should be the thing that finally convinces you to get a blowtorch if you don't already own one. I promise that you won't have buyer's remorse. I make the gianduja custards the day before or the morning of serving, so I have a banked dessert. I caramelize the sugar just before serving. I use Nocciolata spread because it really comes out swinging in the hazelnut department, but Nutella works too.

1   Preheat the oven to 300°F. Place eight 3½-inch ramekins on a large baking dish. Set a kettle of water to boil.

2   In a medium saucepan over medium heat, warm the cream until it's just steaming.

3   Meanwhile, in a large bowl, whisk together the eggs, egg yolks, ½ cup sugar, and salt until the mixture is pale, just a couple of minutes.

4   Gradually pour the warm cream into the egg-sugar mixture, whisking constantly. Then, whisk in the hazelnut-chocolate spread and vanilla.

5   Pour the mixture into the ramekins, about three-fourths full.

6   Place the baking dish in the oven, then carefully pour boiling water into the pan, until it comes halfway up the sides of the ramekins. Bake until the edges of the custards have set but the centers remain jiggly, about 35 minutes. Remove the custards from the water bath. Let cool, then cover the custards with plastic wrap and refrigerate until firm, or up to 2 days.

7   Evenly sprinkle 2 teaspoons sugar over the top of each custard and use a blowtorch to caramelize the sugar. Let them sit for a minute or so, until the sugar hardens before serving.

Pasta,

I'll always want you.

Wreck me, take my waistline, I don't care.

I love that you hate perfect. Perfect is exhausting.

Has anyone told you, you deserve a tablecloth?

Thank you for settling my kids time after time. I owe you.

Thanks for being there when I'm lost at sea, exhausted, on the homestretch, losing patience, restless, teary, feeling foolish… then when I'm partying, celebrating, flirting, laughing my head off, plotting a path, finding the next gear, giddy with excitement, wanting more, more, more… because pasta, you know—I'm not done yet.

You're a good listener.

Why do you smell so good cooking in boiling water?

I'll never not crave you.

Sorry, it's that time of the night when everyone's drunk too much and starts talking stupid.

I'll get to the point.

You're everything to me.

I'm all in.

You belong with me.

The Pasta Toolkit

I could quite happily spend my days in an Italian grocery store. Nothing makes me happier than a basket full of handsome ingredients. I've said it before, and I'll say it again: When you have only a few ingredients in a recipe, you want them to be the best you can get your hands on.

In My Grocery Basket

Aged Gruyère

Aged and white balsamic, red wine, Cabernet Sauvignon, Champagne, Moscatel, and sherry vinegars

Burrata

Butter, salted, unsalted, and European-style with a higher percentage of fat

Cannellini beans and chickpeas

Capers and caperberries

Certified D.O.P. San Marzano canned tomatoes

Crème fraîche

Dried porcini mushrooms

Fontina

French or Greek feta

Guanciale (pig's cheek), pancetta, prosciutto, or Italian sausage

Heavy cream

Kosher and flaky sea salts (especially Maldon)

Mascarpone

Nocciolata hazelnut-cocoa spread

Oil-packed anchovies, tuna, and artichoke hearts

Olives of various varieties

Pecorino, including Romano, Toscano, and Sardo

Real-deal Parmigiano Reggiano with its waxy, lettered rind

Red pepper flakes

Umbrian or Puy lentils

Vanilla beans

Whole black, white, pink, and Kampot peppercorns

Whole-milk ricotta

DRIED PASTAS (AND MY FAVORITE GLUTEN-FREE PASTAS)

Look for bronze-drawn, air-dried pasta. Rustichella d'Abruzzo, Rummo, and Monograno Felicetti are brands that I love, and I can always find the reliable De Cecco, in any shape I need, in every grocery store. I love to have myriad shapes on hand. For gluten-free pastas, I stick with brown rice, buckwheat, and farro pastas made by Jovial, Rustichella d'Abruzzo, and Tinkyáda.

EGGS

Let's talk about eggs; they're important. They add flavor, color, protein, and nutrients to pasta dough and make it luxurious and silky. *Simple Pasta* uses standard-size large eggs that weigh approximately 2 ounces, or 57 grams. To make a dough even *more* luxurious, feel free to use only yolks—no whites. But make sure the weight is equivalent to what's in the recipe. Alternatively, egg white can replace the water in pasta dough.

FRESH PRODUCE

When selecting fresh fruit and vegetables, always check for ripeness. If you are unsure, ask the seller what's best. Buy locally grown produce whenever you can and eat in sync with what each season offers. If you have a garden, plant things that go perfectly with pasta, like zucchini, tomatoes, snap peas, fennel, a variety of lettuces, leafy and woody herbs, chard, spinach, citrus, and edible flowers.

OIL AND WINE

When it comes to oil and wine, I can never have enough. I know the good stuff costs a little more but splurge when you can, since it's an investment in flavor. Extra-virgin olive oil (EVOO) is a bit like wine in that there are many varieties; each type inherits the terroir particular to the region in which the olives are grown. Extra-virgin olive oil is unrefined and made from cold-pressed olives (on a traditional press), whereas regular olive oil is a blend, including both cold-pressed and processed oils. Cold extraction keeps the nutritional value while maintaining the olive's unique qualities. Some EVOOs are made from a single variety of olives, while many are a blend. I tend to use two types: a versatile, neutral oil to cook with, and a more distinct oil for finishing. Before cooking with any EVOO, taste it. Is it pungent, peppery, grassy, bitter, or persistent? Or does it linger with mellow afternotes and subtleties? Think about what you're pairing it with—meat, fish, vegetables, or perhaps dessert? Olive harvest

begins in autumn; when stored in a dark place and sealed from oxygen, the bottle of oil should last for a year (if there is a date of production, it's a clue you're on to a good thing). Like all fruit, olives are best handled with care; look for "hand-picked." I generally buy Italian brands such as Frantoia, Partanna, and Lorenzo, or Californian ones, like California Olive Ranch or Cobram Estate, but there are so many different brands, and discovering them is half the fun.

As for wine, cook with one that's good enough to be consumed on its own . . . ideally when you're cooking the recipe! For deglazing pans, I want a white wine that's not sweet, but is acid-driven with plenty of minerality. If in doubt, stick with Sauvignon Blanc, Vermentino, or pinot grigio. For braising, I like a red that's got a deep inky color and is big on fruit, like Sangiovese, Cabernet Sauvignon, or a full-bodied Nebbiolo.

Types of Flour

I've used many brands and types of flour when making pasta dough. Overall, my general advice for the beginner is to start with an Italian brand of flour, get to know its character, and, if you like it, stick with it—that way you're more likely to get consistent results. As you get more experienced, you can experiment with different brands or create your own blend, using a combination of wheat and non-wheat flours. However, the gluten in wheat flour gives pasta dough structure and elasticity that allows it to be rolled and shaped.

Most gluten-free flour mixtures will cut it for a cake or a cookie but won't work for pasta dough. To mimic the characteristics of gluten, you need to use a combination of flours and starches, as well as more fat and protein, to give the dough structure and elasticity. I experimented with many gluten-free "all-purpose" baking flours but found they tore and broke when rolled. Such flours cannot be used by themselves to make fresh gluten-free pasta dough, except for Caputo Gluten-Free Flour. The following are the flours that I use from most to least often.

TIPO 00 FLOUR

A type of flour made from soft durum wheat, the gold standard for pasta dough, and my number-one choice for homemade pasta. The 00, or double zero, refers to how finely the flour has been ground; 00 flour has a moderately high gluten content. The fine grind of the flour gives pasta a superb, silky mouthfeel.

SEMOLINA FLOUR

A type of flour made from hard durum wheat with a higher gluten content than 00 flour. It's coarser than 00 and all-purpose flour. Once again, stick with Italian brands of semolina flour, like Caputo Semola, Mulino Marino, and De Cecco, that are finely milled and feel only slightly more textured than 00 flour. Semolina flour is often described as soft sand, but don't make the mistake of buying coarse semolina that's more appropriate for pizza making, not for pasta. Semolina gives non-egg-based pasta its yellow color.

ALL-PURPOSE FLOUR

All-purpose flour is a sturdy, reliable choice for homemade pasta if you can't get your hands on 00 flour. The mouthfeel won't be quite as delicate. I usually buy organic, GMO-free, unbleached all-purpose flour.

SPELT FLOUR

An ancient grain, spelt has a wholesome quality and makes a light flour. It still contains gluten but absorbs liquid easily, so those with gluten-free diets may find it easier to digest. If you want a healthier, nutrient-rich flour, spelt is an excellent alternative.

CAPUTO GLUTEN-FREE FLOUR

My enthusiasm for this flour blend cannot be overstated. While it's designed for making gluten-free pizza and bread, I've found it works wonderfully in pasta as well. You'll never know it's gluten-free! It's amazing for cut shapes, noodles, and filled pastas; has a lovely mouthfeel, isn't grainy or dry; and tastes like wheat-based pasta. It can be purchased online or at specialty food markets. Gluten-free pasta dough needs to be rolled out by hand with a rolling pin a few times until it's thin enough to be easily fed through pasta rollers. This stops it from crumbling and tearing.

Pasta Tools

Pasta can be made with only a fork, wooden board, rolling pin, and sharp knife, but here are a few tools I've found to be very helpful.

BENCH SCRAPER

Use to bring dough together, clean your wooden work surface, and transfer delicate, filled pasta shapes and gnocchi into cooking water.

DIGITAL SCALE

The most accurate way to measure flour and eggs and to get consistent results. Buy one!

FOOD PROCESSOR

Bring pasta dough together, make pestos and fillings for stuffed pastas, or puree sauces in minutes.

HAND-CRANKED PASTA ROLLER

Affordable and transportable. Mine often travels with me. I recommend a Marcato Atlas or the Imperia pasta machines.

KITCHENAID STAND MIXER WITH PASTA ACCESSORIES

Not essential but a game changer! Bring together pasta dough in minutes using a paddle attachment. The pasta-rolling attachments roll and cut pasta very quickly. Invaluable for making pasta on a weeknight. I use mine ALL THE TIME and encourage you to do the same.

PAN FOR PASTA

To finesse and finish pasta perfectly, a lightweight pan with sloped sides that conducts heat well (at least 11 inches in diameter and 3¾ inches deep) will become one of your most used vessels. It should be large enough (3 to 4 quarts) to toss the pasta easily.

PASTA AND RAVIOLI CUTTERS OR COOKIE CUTTERS

Use ravioli cutters, which have a sharp metal outline that cut the dough well. If you don't have ravioli cutters, cookie cutters will work. A fluted pasta or pastry cutter creates a lovely decorative edge. Round cookie cutters in various sizes also help shape the filling and remove trapped air.

PIPING BAG

Fill pastas easily and evenly with a piping bag (a plastic bag with a corner snipped off also does the trick).

RICER OR BOX GRATER

Pass cooked potatoes through a ricer to achieve the ultra-smooth texture needed for potato gnocchi. Alternatively, grate cooked potatoes on the finest side of a box grater or a Microplane. The box grater is also, of course, just the thing for grating mountains of cheese.

RULER

You can cut rolled pasta easily and accurately if you use a ruler.

SMALL DOWEL OR PENCIL

Use a small dowel or a pencil to roll cylindrical pasta shapes such as garganelli.

SPIDER

Strain and transfer cooked pasta into sauces easily with a large wire spider. It also ensures that you always have starchy pasta water remaining.

SPRAY BOTTLE

Hydrate pasta dough with an even, light mist of water from a spray bottle if the dough starts to dry out during the shaping and filling process.

WOODEN BOARD

Ideally, designate one large wooden cutting board exclusively for making pasta, so no unwanted flavors or smells are absorbed. Rolling pasta by hand requires a large untreated wooden board that's about 4 by 3 feet. Look for porous woods, like poplar and linden, that add a wonderful texture to the pasta. Don't wet the board to clean it. Instead, use a bench scraper to thoroughly remove any remaining dough. To store, cover the board with a clean cotton cloth.

WOODEN GNOCCHI BOARD

Using a wooden gnocchi board gives the dough decorative ridges that will help sauces cling to the pasta.

WOODEN ROLLING PIN

If you don't have pasta-rolling accessories or a hand-cranked roller, you'll need a rolling pin to roll out pasta dough. A standard rolling pin works in a pinch, but you'll need to work with smaller pieces of dough. Ideally, you'll want a mattarello, a thin, wooden rolling pin that's about 40 inches long, to roll very large sheets of pasta. You can find beautiful vintage ones online.

Acknowledgments

It takes a village, and that's the best part about writing a cookbook.

I'm going to start with my husband, Nick; my love, cheerleader, and constant support. Thank you for always encouraging me to do my best work. You always keep life fun and interesting, even under pressure. There is no one else I'd rather have my gin and tonic with. I love you.

The kiddos, Opal, Ned, Dixie, and Matilda. Thanks for loving dinnertime as much as me.

Thank you, Kari Stuart and Catherine Shook at ICM for the continued guidance and unwavering support.

Team Ten Speed Press: Kelly Snowden, my editor and food soul mate. Thank you for suggesting pasta. It was an excellent idea. Emma Campion, for always fostering the best creative direction. You both are such a pleasure to work with. A big thank-you to Hannah Rahill, Kim Keller, Zoey Brandt, Dolores York, and Sohayla Farman for the fine tuning.

My crew, Team Jans: Nikole Herriott, Michael Graydon, Amy Elise Wilson, Rebecca Jurkevich, and Cybelle Tondu. Wow! I could not have asked for a more magic squad. Thank you for making the photoshoots so memorable, the exquisite work, and friendship. It was collaboration at its best. Grazie for making *Simple Pasta* the best book it could be.

Mikaela Martin, for capturing all the behind-the-scenes photos. You have the eye and empathy of an actor. It's refreshing to see the world through your lens. Brett Stiller, for being a ray of light, cooking up a storm with me, laughing our heads off, and always having wise counsel.

Marisa Dobson, it always starts with you, putting my ideas in order.

Airyka Rockerfeller, what a joy it was cooking, recipe testing, and putting nascent ideas down on random scraps of paper that would develop into fully conceived recipes. Your knowledge in the kitchen is equally rivaled with your editor's eye. How special it was working together.

Rachel Tervenski, for bringing fresh and classic design to all things OW and this book.

Sfoglina Julia Ficara from Grano & Farina cooking school in Rome, for being an excellent teacher and giving thoughtful feedback to the manuscript. (When in Rome, one must go and learn from a pro!)

Michael Whidden, for all the wine recommendations. I don't know what I loved more, learning from you or tasting the wine!

Simon D'Arcy, who cooks for fifty like it was five, thank for your putting your culinary expertise toward this book.

Deborah Lloyd, Amy Lyons, Megara Vogl, Ellie Bowman Backer, and Tara Mark, for putting the recipes through their paces.

Anna Sordo and her mother, Alba, the one and only legend that is Mama Sordo, for sharing family recipes and for keeping me fed in college.

My sister-in-law Michelle Aluqdah, for keeping me physically in shape and sane while I wrote a pasta cookbook.

Vivi, our host in Marsala, Sicily. Shooting at the villa was a dream. I will always have an image of you playing with your grandson under the shade of the citrus trees. May I come back as one of your grandchildren?

About the Author

Odette Williams is an Australian cook and writer with a simple, effortless, and approachable style. She is the author of Amazon Editor's Pick *Simple Cake*, which was named one of the best baking cookbooks of 2019 by the *New York Times*. Odette's eponymous brand has been sold at Goop, Anthropologie, J.Crew, ABC Carpet & Home, Le Bon Marché, and other retailers. Odette writes for the *Wall Street Journal*, and her work and writing have been featured in *Rachael Ray In Season*, *Vogue*, *InStyle*, *Martha Stewart Living*, *Real Simple*, *Parents*, *Southern Living*, and *Saveur* and by Food Network. Odette lives in Brooklyn with her husband and two children.

Index

Published in the United States by Ten Speed Press, an imprint of
Random House, a division of Penguin Random House LLC, New York.
TenSpeed.com
RandomHouseBooks.com

Ten Speed Press and the Ten Speed Press colophon are registered
trademarks of Penguin Random House LLC.

Typeface(s): DJR's Forma DJR Mircro, ITC's Souvenir,
and Newlyn's New Spirit

Library of Congress Control Number: 2022934786

Hardcover ISBN: 978-1-9848-5992-1
eBook ISBN: 978-1-9848-5993-8

Printed in China

Page 70: Garlic bread styled by Christopher St. Onge.

Acquiring editor: Kelly Snowden | Developmental editor: Kim Keller
Production editor: Sohayla Farman
Designer: Rachel Tervenski
Design Manager: Emma Campion
Production designers: Mari Gill and Faith Hague
Production manager: Serena Sigona
Prepress color manager: Jane Chinn
Food stylist: Rebecca Jurkevich | Food stylist assistant: Cybelle Tondu
Prop stylist: Amy Elise Wilson
Copyeditor: Dolores York | Proofreader: Adaobi Obi Tulton
Indexer: Amy Hall
Publicist: Kristin Casemore | Marketer: Andrea Portanova

10 9 8 7 6 5 4 3 2 1

First Edition